OXFORD
UNIVERSITY PRESS

Fiona Beddall • Kenna Bourke

Blue Dot 6

Workbook

1 What can happen when we imitate?

A **Read and complete the recipe.**

fry   dough   properly   stir   technique   mixture

Cookie Recipe

The most popular [1] __________ for making cookies is probably to bake them in the oven, but this recipe uses an interesting alternative method.

Put the flour and sugar in a bowl, and add some milk and vanilla extract to the [2] __________ .

Next, [3] __________ with a wooden spoon until there are no lumps.

Roll the [4] __________ until it's 1 cm thick, and cut into circles with a glass.

Finally, [5] __________ the circles in oil. When they're brown on one side, turn them over so they can cook [6] __________ on the other side, too.

B **Match the sentences.**

1 My favorite restaurant was closed, so we couldn't eat there.

2 He didn't want to eat the food.

3 The food needed more flavor.

4 We had a salad of white cheese, black olives, green lettuce, red tomatoes, orange and yellow peppers, and purple cabbage.

5 There were some potatoes in the cabinet.

6 She made a spicy curry for the contest.

a It looked disgusting.

b We decided to add some herbs.

c What a shame!

d We love multicolored food.

e The judges loved it!

f We cooked and mashed them and ate them with some fish.

A **Complete the sentences with the adjective form of these words.**

> storm   mess   taste   spice   thirst

1 I've just been playing tennis with my friend and I feel really _________________ now!

2 This is a great restaurant, they do a really _________________ spinach and ricotta lasagne.

3 Have you tried this red curry? I think I need a drink, it's too _________________ for me!

4 It was a very _________________ night and a lot of branches fell in our yard.

5 Why haven't you cleaned up your room yet? It's so _________________ in there.

B **Write the correct verb tense. Write *going to*, *will*, or *present continuous*.**

1 Don't be nervous about the presentation. You'll be fine. _________________

2 I'm meeting my teacher at 10:30 tomorrow morning. _________________

3 How old will your sister be next year? _________________

4 We're hiking in the mountains with our cousins next summer. _________________

5 I think there's going to be a storm later – look at those dark clouds! _________________

6 My friends aren't going to the beach next weekend. _________________

C **Read the sentences. Write sentences using *going to* to make predictions.**

> be a hot day   go on vacation   get wet   have a picnic

1 It's only 6:00 a.m. and it's already warm in the yard!

It _________________________________.

2 Dad is putting sandwiches in a bag.

We _________________________________.

3 Watch out! There's a big puddle.

You _________________________________.

4 I see my cousin packing her suitcase.

She _________________________________.

1   Our team is playing in the final tomorrow. _______________________

2   I'm playing piano in a concert tomorrow. _______________________

3   Winter is coming. _______________________

4   We're finishing sixth grade soon. _______________________

5   I can't think of a plot for my story. _______________________

6   My tablet isn't working. _______________________

E **Write sentences about the summer camp schedule. Use the present continuous.**

Summer Camp!

Sunday	arrive at camp 10:00 a.m.
Monday	learn to put up a tent
Tuesday	explore the forest
Wednesday	cook breakfast on the campfire
Thursday	swim in the lake
Friday	do a storytelling contest

1   They're arriving at the camp on Sunday. _______________________

2   _______________________

3   _______________________

4   _______________________

5   _______________________

6   _______________________

F **Write questions with the future tenses in parentheses.**

1   What / you / do / later today (present continuous)

____

2   When / you / go / on vacation / this year (present continuous)

____

3   Where / you / go / next weekend (will)

____

4   What / you / do / this weekend (going to)

____

A **Read the story. How does Nadine surprise her friends?**

A Challenge from Chantal!

Nadine and Chantal were walking home from school, discussing food from around the world. Nadine was an enthusiastic cook. She enjoyed nothing more than stirring, frying, or mashing ingredients to make special dishes for her family and friends.

"How did you learn to make pizza, Nadine?" asked Chantal. "Your pizza is the best I've ever tasted!"

"That's kind of you," replied Nadine. "But my pizza isn't really mine. I copied the technique from my cousin, Luc. He has a pizza delivery business!"

"It's still totally delicious!" said Chantal, licking her lips. "And where did you learn to make that creamy sauce we had at your home last weekend?"

"The creamy mushroom sauce? I copied that from a really cool TV chef. I'd copy everything she did, … if Mom and Dad would let me!"

Chantal smiled. "You've done enough copying. Everyone knows you're a great cook, maybe even a great chef! You can invent your own recipe! Go on, I challenge you to invent a dish no one has tasted before."

"OK," grinned Nadine. "I will!"

Two weeks later, Nadine came to class with 29 envelopes, one for each classmate. Inside the envelopes was an invitation.

That Saturday, all of Nadine's classmates arrived for the party. They were excited to find out what the mystery dish was.

"I think it's a pizza," whispered Pierre to his friend, Yves.

"No, it's a cake," replied Yves.

"No way," said Chantal. "I'm sure it's going to be more sophisticated than a cake. It might be … chicken in Nadine's famous creamy sauce!"

"But that would be easy to guess," argued Michelle.

"You're right. We'll just have to find out," agreed Chantal. And they all rushed into the kitchen. In the middle of the table was a delicious looking dessert with a multicolored top and creamy middle, sat on top of baked cookie dough!

"Yay! Pizza!" yelled Pierre. "I was right!"

"No, it isn't pizza," smiled Nadine.

"It looks like pizza," said Yves.

"Have a taste." Nadine cut a slice for everyone.

"Wow! It's delicious!" said Chantal, licking her lips.

"Correct! First, I made cookie dough and baked it. Next, I spread cream on top. Finally, I arranged the fruits and berries. I'm naming it *Imitation Pizza*!"

Nadine turned to cut more slices, but the dessert was already gone.

B **Underline these words in the text.**

> frying   multicolored   mashing   technique   stirring   dough

C **Check (✓) the correct answer.**

1 How does Nadine learn new dishes at the beginning of the story?

☐ She uses her imagination. ☐ She copies other people.

2 How does Chantal know Nadine can cook?

☐ She's tried Nadine's pizza and creamy sauce. ☐ Nadine's cousin, Luc, told her.

3 What's in the creamy sauce Nadine copied from a TV chef?

☐ cream, fruit, and berries ☐ cream and mushrooms

4 What does Chantal challenge Nadine to do?

☐ have a pizza party ☐ invent a dish

5 Who does Nadine invite to her "Guess the Dish Party"?

☐ all her classmates ☐ Chantal and her parents

6 What does Nadine make for the "Guess the Dish Party"?

☐ a sweet dish ☐ a savory dish

D **When Nadine made her *Imitation Pizza*, what were the three steps in the process?**

1 _______________________________________

2 _______________________________________

3 _______________________________________

A **Complete the sentences.**

> animation   setting   evil   depth   illustrations
> influence   facial expression   villain

1   To calculate the ______________ of the swimming pool, measure from the bottom to the top.

2   I can see from your ______________ that you're angry about something.

3   The story's ______________ was a desert island.

4   There is often a ______________ in crime and detective stories.

5   We watched a fantastic ______________ in class today!

6   Advertisements sometimes ______________ people to buy things they don't need.

7   In most traditional stories there is a good character and an ______________ character.

8   There are no ______________ in this book, so you have to use your imagination.

B **Read and circle the correct option.**

I just wrote a great story! It's about a [1] **facial expression** / **villain** named Sir Albatross.
He has the power to [2] **influence** / **evil** people. He can also scare his enemies just by using
a frightening [3] **depth** / **facial expression**. All the characters in my story know that Sir Albatross
is [4] **evil** / **illustration**, and they want to stop him. The [5] **setting** / **animation** for my story is
a dark forest in the winter. My teacher likes my story a lot. She thinks one day someone could
make an [6] **influence** / **animation** from it. I drew an [7] **illustration** / **influence** of Sir Albatross
and I'm going to show it to her!

A **Check (✓) the correct option.**

1 If you want to change something about your town or city, you need to talk to the … .

☐ environmental ☐ council

2 If you're a street artist, you might draw on the sidewalk with … .

☐ population ☐ chalk

3 If you want other people to take action, you might start a … .

☐ chalk ☐ campaign

4 If you're talking about all the people who live in a place, you talk about the … .

☐ population ☐ eager

5 If you're feeling enthusiastic about something, people might say you're … .

☐ eager ☐ campaign

6 If you're interested in … issues, you care about the natural world.

☐ council ☐ environmental

B **Complete the sentences.**

chalk   environmental   campaign   population   council   eager

1 When my parents were at school, their teachers used to write on the board with _______________ . But nowadays we have digital interactive boards instead.

2 Some of my neighbors began a _______________ to get more entertainment spaces in our town. Now our town _______________ has plans to build a new park and playground.

3 Most of the _______________ in my country cares a lot about _______________ problems. We're all _______________ to do what we can to reduce waste.

What environmental campaigns are you eager to get involved with?

1

A **Check (✓) the sentences with a connector that expresses a contrast. Underline the connector.**

1. ☐ Unlike all my brothers and sisters, I have blue eyes.

2. ☐ I'm very good at languages. However, I'm not so good at math.

3. ☐ Both my parents are scientists. My aunt is a doctor.

4. ☐ I eat a lot of vegetables, whereas my sister prefers fruit.

5. ☐ I don't really like oranges. However, I love grapefruit!

6. ☐ Mom enjoys cooking. Dad also cooks delicious meals every day.

B **Complete the sentences with *however*, *whereas*, or *unlike*.**

1. I enjoy singing and dancing, _______________ my brother likes reading and sports.

2. I like salsa music, too. _______________ , I find salsa dancing tiring!

3. _______________ my brother, I don't like sports at all!

4. I don't enjoy painting. _______________ , I do many other activities, like cooking, for example.

5. I discovered that making a salad is easy, _______________ making pasta isn't.

6. _______________ Dad, I love all kinds of Italian food. Dad only likes Mexican food.

C **Write a paragraph about something you're good at. Use connectors to express a contrast.**

My older brother is really good at skateboarding, whereas I'm not! Every time I've tried skateboarding, I've fallen over. However, I am very good at spelling. I love to look in the dictionary and find new words – long words are my favorite ones!

One of the first long words I learned to spell was "Wednesday." It's a fun word because it looks like Wed-Nes-Day. However, you don't need to pronounce the first "D."

____

____

____

____

A Unscramble the words to complete the paragraph.

I really wanted to learn how to cook Italian food [1] p______________ (prlyerop), so I asked my grandmother to teach me. Yesterday, I learned to make a [2] m______________ (remixut) of eggs, flour, and water to make pasta. Grandma let me [3] s______________ (rist) it all together to make a [4] d______________ (ughod). Before it's cooked it tastes [5] d______________ (tidisggusn), so don't try it! Next, I learned how to [6] f______________ (yfr) chicken gently in a pan. We added some [7] h______________ (behrs) to make it tasty. It was really good! Next, I want to know what [8] t______________ (quenitech) to use for making pizza!

B Circle the word that is different.

1	fry	mash	influence
2	eager	salty	tasty
3	villain	chalk	evil
4	shame	animation	illustration
5	campaign	properly	council
6	mixture	dough	depth

C Read and circle the correct option.

A: What plans do you have this weekend?

B: I have exciting plans! I [1] **'m having** / **will have** a sleepover at my cousin's house. My aunt and uncle [2] **will pick** / **are picking** me up at 4:00 p.m. on Friday.

A: When [3] **are you getting** / **will you get** to their house?

B: Around five.

A: What [4] **will you do** / **are you going to do** with your cousin?

B: On Saturday morning we [5] **'re seeing** / **will see** a new action movie. Then we're going to a soccer game in the afternoon.

Think and Reflect: Unit 1

The most interesting thing that I learned ______________________________________

My understanding of imitation ☆ ☆ ☆ ☆ ☆

My goal for Unit 2 ______________________________________

Vocabulary 1

A Complete the sentences.

> come up with   require   barely   disturb   backward   emerged

1 He did a ______________ dive into the pool.

2 Pets ______________ a lot of care.

3 They often ______________ fantastic ideas.

4 Mom was working so I wasn't allowed to ______________ her.

5 I took this photo when the dolphins ______________ from the water.

6 The food was ______________ edible, but I managed to eat a little.

B Match to make sentences.

1 He got a medal …   **a** when he jumped into the water.

2 There were springs …   **b** for winning the race.

3 He made a splash …   **c** of thunder.

4 When there was a curve …   **d** in the trampoline to make it bouncy.

5 There was a big boom …   **e** the spaceship into space.

6 They launched …   **f** in the road, the car slowed down.

A **Complete the sentences with the noun form of one of the verbs in parentheses. Use the suffix _-ment_.**

1 There was a lot of ___excitement___ about the new recreation center. (excite / treat)

2 The jacket is too big, but with an _______________ at the shoulders, it will fit better. (argue / adjust)

3 Your invention has won an international design competition. What a fantastic _______________! (achieve / agree)

4 We have to find a way to control the _______________ of the robot's hands more accurately. (move / develop)

5 At first we had very different ideas, but we reached an _______________ in the end. (achieve / agree)

6 The _______________ of a safe solar-powered plane is taking longer than we expected. (move / develop)

7 We both got really angry and we had an _______________ about our project. (argue / adjust)

8 The new _______________ for this disease will help people to recover more quickly. (excite / treat)

B **Complete the chart with the continuous forms of the verbs.**

	Positive	Negative	Question
1	They're speaking.	They aren't speaking.	_______________
2	_______________	_______________	Am I running?
3	_______________	You weren't lying.	_______________
4	She was listening.	_______________	_______________
5	_______________	We haven't been waiting.	_______________
6	_______________	_______________	Has it been raining?

C **Read and circle the correct option.**

Alfred Fielding and Marc Chavannes
1 were trying / have been trying to create plastic wallpaper when they invented bubble wrap. No one has ever used it as wallpaper, but people **2 are using / have been using** it to protect delicate things for over sixty years. At the moment, I **3 'm putting / 've been putting** it around our favorite picture frames before we move home.

bubble wrap

 Unscramble the sentences.

1 been / for months / She / has / working / on her idea

____

2 photographing / you / the / Were / when they flew away / bees / ?

____

3 been / Have / improving / invention / they / their / ?

____

4 wasn't / results / The / positive / expecting / scientist

____

 Complete the dialogues with the continuous forms of the verbs.

read

A: What [1] _______________ you _______________ ?

B: A book about inventions. I got it out of the library this afternoon,
and I [2] _______________________ it ever since.
I [3] _______________________ it when you came home three
hours ago, and I [4] _______________ still _______________ it now.

sleep

A: I can't find Sofia. She [5] _______________ not _______________
in her bedroom. Do you know where she is?

B: She [6] _____________________ in her tree tent. She
[7] _____________________ there last night, too. In fact,
she [8] _____________________ there every night this week.

 Answer the questions about you.

1 What are you doing right now? _________________________________

2 What were you doing three hours ago? ___________________________

3 What has been happening at your school this week? _________________

4 Who was sitting next to you in class yesterday? ___________________

5 What have you been studying in science recently? ___________________

6 What are you wearing today? _________________________________

A **Read the website article. How are the plants in the three sections the same?**

Plant Power

Animals have given inventors inspiration for a huge variety of amazing technology. But what about plants? They do things differently from animals, but they too have incredible problem-solving designs. Here are a few of the cool things that we're learning from the greener species on our planet.

Wings like a seed's

Birds and insects aren't the only species with wings. Trees such as maples produce seeds with wings, too. As the seeds fall to the ground, the wings start to spin. This helps the seeds to travel further from the parent tree and find somewhere good to grow.

Maple seed wings have provided a fantastic learning opportunity for engineers. Copying their special shape has helped people to design blades for wind turbines that can cut through the air more smoothly. This helps wind turbines to produce more electricity – great news for the fight against climate change!

a lotus plant

Like water off a lotus

Lotus plants grow in lakes and shallow rivers. Their stems are underwater, but their leaves and beautiful flowers emerge above the water. To thrive, lotuses require the right amount of carbon dioxide, which is absorbed through the leaves. Water or mud on the leaves can disturb the process. But that isn't a problem, because the leaves have a special bumpy surface that makes splashes of water roll off them immediately. Any dirt rolls off with the water.

One group of scientists have imitated the lotus leaf's design to protect metal from rust. And others are trying to use similar technology to create solar panels that can clean themselves. Cleaner panels can produce more electricity, so, just like the better wind turbines, they will help in our fight to reduce climate change.

As strong as a cucumber

There are many strong animals. Elephants can push over trees, and one beetle species can push an object more than a thousand times heavier than its own body weight! But plants are strong, too. A cucumber plant has tiny curly stems called tendrils. Tendrils twist around other plants and help the cucumber plant climb toward the sun. These twisting stems can pull the plant upward even when there are big, heavy cucumbers hanging from it.

Scientists have figured out how the tendrils grow in a curve that twists and grabs other plants. And engineers have used this knowledge to come up with a new type of robot. It can lift things 650 times its own weight!

B **Underline these words in the text.**

> require   splashes   come up with   emerge   curve   disturb

C **Analyze the visuals in the article and answer the questions.**

1   What shape are the seeds of maple trees?   _______________________

2   What parts of a wind turbine move round in the wind?   _______________________

3   What color are the lotus flowers?   _______________________

4   What color is rust, and where can you find it?   _______________________

5   Are cucumber tendrils thick or thin?   _______________________

D **Read and circle *True* or *False*.**

1   Plants have designs that solve problems.   True   False

2   A maple seed's wings give it a better chance of becoming a tree.   True   False

3   We can get more electricity from wind turbines if their design imitates maple seeds.   True   False

4   Lotus plants are healthier when their leaves have water and mud on them.   True   False

5   Lotus leaves have helped some scientists to design better wind turbines.   True   False

6   Cucumber tendrils are strong enough to lift a plant with cucumbers on it.   True   False

7   A robot inspired by plant tendrils can lift 650 cucumbers.   True   False

> **What other plants have interesting designs that people could imitate? Why might this be useful?**

A **Three of the four options are correct. Cross out (X) the wrong option.**

1 What can you make from clay?

  a a statue **b** a cup **c** a bowl **d** a window

2 What might have a steering wheel?

  a a bike **b** a ship **c** a car **d** a truck

3 What might be in a coil?

  a a rope **b** a snake **c** a dog **d** a spring

4 What can you mold?

  a clay **b** water **c** bread dough **d** mud

5 What does a cart usually need?

  a wheels **b** a horse **c** wings **d** a driver

6 Where does a sailor work?

  a a boat **b** a factory **c** the ocean **d** a ship

B **Read and complete the paragraph.**

> led to   cart   sailor   pottery   mold   coil   clay

The [1] ________________ steered the boat down the river. He thought about the [2] ________________ pots, plates, and statues that he was transporting. His home town had many people who could [3] ________________ clay into useful [4] ________________ and beautiful objects, and he was hoping to sell these products for a lot of money in the big city. But before that, he could enjoy the journey. There were roads that [5] ________________ the city, too, but he had no interest in traveling by horse and [6] ________________ . The views on the river were breathtaking.

He saw a food seller on the river bank and suddenly felt hungry. He picked up a [7] ________________ of rope and threw it toward the bank. It was time for some lunch.

Imagine you were on the boat transporting pottery. What were you doing? How were you feeling?

Vocabulary 3

A Check (✓) the correct option.

1 I've … these clothes now.
- ☐ established
- ☐ grown out of

2 I always wear a … when I go surfing.
- ☐ set
- ☐ wetsuit

3 There's too much … in my bedroom.
- ☐ wetsuit
- ☐ stuff

4 We don't want the spider here, but we don't want to … it.
- ☐ harm
- ☐ grow out of

5 My aunt gave me a nice paint … last week.
- ☐ set
- ☐ stuff

6 They've decided to … a Ping-Pong club at school. I can't wait to join!
- ☐ harm
- ☐ establish

B Read and complete the dialogue.

grown out of   wetsuit   harm   establish   set   stuff

Dad: Hey, Alfie, can you play with your little brother, please? He wants you to put on your **1** _______________ and pretend you're exploring the ocean with him.

Alfie: Oh, Dad, do I have to? I've **2** _______________ it, so it's really uncomfortable.

Dad: OK. Maybe you could play together with your **3** _______________ of plastic bricks.

Alfie: I don't know, Dad. He broke my robot when I let him play with it. I don't want him to damage any more of my **4** _______________ .

Dad: Just **5** _______________ some clear rules, so he knows what he can and can't do. I'm sure he won't **6** _______________ your plastic bricks. They're impossible to break!

A **Match to make sentences.**

1 A paragraph is …
2 Start a new paragraph when you …
3 Don't forget to …
4 Paragraphs make your writing …

a indent each new paragraph.
b a group of sentences that describes one idea.
c clearer, and help your readers to think about what they've read.
d move to a new idea.

B **Draw arrows to mark where the break and the indents should be.**

indent

break

indent

Wheels are everywhere! They are found on vehicles, in factory machines, on rollerblades, and under suitcases. It's hard to imagine a world without them. Different materials are used to make wheels for different purposes. Vehicle wheels are often made of metal, and they're surrounded by tires with air inside. However, toys often have plastic wheels, because they're lighter and cheaper.

C **Write three paragraphs about an interesting animal. Explain what it is, its special abilities, and what humans might learn from it.**

Fireflies are a group of beetles that have wings. They live in a lot of different places in the world.

They're interesting to humans because they have the ability to glow in the dark. Some species glow only when they are babies and have no wings. Other species can glow as adults, too. They fly around and fill the dark with little dots of light.

By studying fireflies, humans might learn how to make light bulbs that use less electricity. This could help us to fight climate change.

A **Read and circle the correct option.**

If you carry heavy [1] **curve / stuff / spring** in a backpack for a long time, it can [2] **harm / establish / emerge** your back. However, if you transport it in a wheeled suitcase, you [3] **coil / boom / barely** notice how much it weighs. So why did humans drive a wheeled vehicle on the moon before anyone [4] **came up with / grew out of / led to** the idea of a wheeled suitcase? It's a mystery!

B **Unscramble the words to complete the sentences.**

1   My new invention is going to l________________ ________________ (d l a e o t) better lives for everyone!

2   You can change direction by turning the s________________ ________________ (g t e r s i n e h e l w e).

3   They used the clay to make some p________________ (p r y t o t e).

4   It's my ambition to win a hockey m________________ (d l m e a) at the Olympic Games.

5   You should wear a w________________ (t e w u i s t) when you go surfing.

6   I've g________________ ________________ ________________ (o w g n r t o u f o) these pants.

C **Correct the mistakes in the underlined parts of these sentences.**

1   <u>He's being making</u> pots on a pottery wheel all day.   ________________

2   Are you waiting for a bus? Where <u>you are going</u>?   ________________

3   <u>I were trying</u> to help, but I made the situation worse.   ________________

4   What <u>were you do</u> yesterday at five thirty?   ________________

5   <u>I not enjoying</u> this cold weather. I hope it'll be warmer soon.   ________________

6   Your hair is wet. <u>Have you be swiming</u>?   ________________

Think and Reflect: Unit 2

My understanding of imitation ☆☆☆☆☆

How well I achieved my goal for Unit 2 ☆☆☆☆☆

The most interesting thing that I learned ________________________________

My goal for Unit 3 ________________________________

Vocabulary 1

A Read and circle the correct option.

1 Remember to lock the door when you leave. This area has a bad **counterfeit** / **reputation**, so you can't **trust** / **bargain** everyone. The building has to be **genuine** / **secure** at night.

2 Our computer was doing **counterfeit** / **weird** things, like sending emails to people when we didn't ask it to. We used an app to check it for **malware** / **reputation**, and **deleted** / **weird** anything that shouldn't be there.

3 I dropped a glass bottle yesterday and it **suspected** / **shattered** into hundreds of pieces. Unfortunately, it also **damaged** / **trusted** the floor, so we'll need someone to fix that.

B Read and complete the dialogue.

counterfeits   genuine   shatter   weird   bargain   secure   reputation   suspect

A: Hey, this website is selling RX5 tablets at reduced prices!

B: Really? RX5s have a great [1] _______________ – everyone says they're fantastic. Their screens never [2] _______________ if you drop them, and they have good software for keeping your information [3] _______________ . How much can you buy one for?

A: $30. It's such a [4] _______________ !

B: Yes, but is it [5] _______________ that it's so cheap? [6] _______________ RX5s usually cost about $200. The ones on that website look like RX5s, but if they're available for only $30, I [7] _______________ they're [8] _______________ . I don't think you should buy one.

A **Circle the correct option.**

1 I should start **doing** / **making** my homework.

2 Where can I **charge** / **power** my phone? The battery is dead, so I need to plug it in somewhere.

3 You **succeeded** / **passed** the test! Congratulations!

4 If you want to play that game on your phone, you'll have to **send** / **download** the app.

5 You need to **say** / **tell** sorry for being so unkind.

6 I've **done** / **made** a terrible mistake.

7 I think we should **give** / **provide** her a present.

8 Be careful that you don't **start** / **set** your hair on fire with that candle!

B **Check (✓) the sentences that use the future continuous with *will* or *going to*.**

1 ☐ This time tomorrow, I'm going to be playing in a soccer game.

2 ☐ We'll be late if we don't hurry.

3 ☐ He won't be meeting his friends this evening.

4 ☐ Will they be having a meal together later?

5 ☐ You're going to have a great time.

6 ☐ She's going to be staying in a nice apartment.

C **Unscramble the sentences.**

1 to / going / be / tomorrow / helping / I'm / you

____

2 be / Your / phone / working / will / soon

____

3 won't / They / learning / Arabic / be

____

4 we / be / When / camping / will / ?

____

5 She / swimming / is / going / to / not / be

____

6 the show / be / Are / you / watching / to / going / ?

____

1   We will discussing our ideas tonight.

<u>We will be discussing our ideas tonight.</u>

2   They're going be writing stories in their next English lesson.

____

3   At this time tomorrow, he's going to be run in a race.

____

4   Will you be stayed here for long?

____

5   We not going to be playing games with our grandparents tomorrow afternoon.

____

6   I won't to be doing the project on Saturday.

____

E Complete the future continuous sentences. Use the verbs in parentheses.

1   Where will you ________ <u>be waiting</u> ________ when I get there? (wait)

We ______________________ on the bench in the square. (sit)

2   Are they going to ______________________ in the mountains next week? (ski)

No, they aren't. They ______________________ . (hike)

3   What is she ______________________ on her vacation? (do)

She ______________________ . (surf)

4   When will you ______________________ past my house? (walk)

At 7:00 a.m., I ______________________ to go to school. So around five minutes later. (leave)

F Read and complete the paragraph with the future continuous form of these verbs.

not join in   sing   cook   celebrate   plan   take   dance

This time tomorrow, we [1] ______________________ the New Year.
My cousins and I [2] ______________________ to our favorite music,
and we [3] ______________________ loudly, too! My brother
[4] ______________________ with the dancing. I expect he
[5] ______________________ photos of us all. My mom and dad
[6] ______________________ some nice food for us, and my aunt
[7] ______________________ some silly games. I can't wait!

What will you be doing at this time tomorrow?

A **Read the journal entries. What does Aimee achieve?**

Aimee's Journal

Monday, October 30

My friends couldn't believe that my new phone set a newspaper on fire! 🔥

They said I was lucky it didn't damage the house. And everyone's wondering if their own devices are genuine or not. They're going to talk to their parents about where the devices were bought, and check for malware.

Our teacher, Mr. Park, heard us talking about the fire.

"Why don't you give the whole school a presentation about the dangers of counterfeits?" he said. But I can't do that. I hate speaking in front of a lot of people.

Tuesday, November 6

There was a sad story on the local news today. A baby is in the hospital because he ate a battery from a bad-quality counterfeit toy. 🙁

Since I heard that, I've been thinking again about Mr. Park's suggestion. It's really important to make more people aware of this issue. Maybe I should be brave and give that presentation.

Wednesday, November 7

My presentation is all arranged. In one week, I'm going to be speaking in front of the whole school! Help! 😰

Mr. Park says you feel less nervous if you're really well prepared, so I've spent this evening doing research and planning my presentation. Mom has promised to help me practice.

Tuesday, November 13

I've been practicing all week, and I think I'm ready for tomorrow's presentation. Mr. Park has even invited the local news station! I feel really nervous, but I'll be giving people an important message, so nothing's going to stop me!

Wednesday, November 14

I did it! My presentation went really well. Everyone says they're going to tell their families how to avoid buying counterfeit items products in the future. And they're going to report websites to the police if they suspect they might be selling counterfeit items. After the presentation, I did an interview with a TV reporter. It'll be weird to see myself on tonight's TV news, but it'll really help the campaign. I'm going to give my presentation at other local schools soon, too.

I received a letter today with some amazing news: thanks to my campaign, the police have stopped the sale of thousands of counterfeit products! Local people have been giving the police a lot more information than before my campaign started. And that's helped the police to find the places where the counterfeits were stored – including some products that were really dangerous. People are safer now because of my campaign! 😓

B **Underline these words in the text.**

damage   counterfeits   malware   suspect   genuine   weird

C **Number the events in the correct order.**

a ☐ Aimee finds out that her campaign has had a positive result.

b ☐ Aimee agrees to Mr. Park's suggestion.

c ☐ Aimee's phone starts a fire.

d ☐ Aimee gives her presentation.

e ☐ Aimee finds out about someone else who was put in danger by a counterfeit product.

f ☐ Aimee is interviewed by a TV reporter.

D ⚙ **Answer the questions about Aimee.**

1   What does she like or dislike?

____

2   What do her words and actions tell you about her?

____

3   How do other people feel about her?

____

4   How does she change? Why?

____

A **Match to make sentences.**

1 Creatures such as …
2 Your flesh …
3 Prey …
4 Species evolve …
5 Camouflage …
6 A sudden change …

a is between your skin …
b to help them …
c is eaten …
d happens …
e butterflies have …
f makes animals …

g quickly.
h by predators.
i difficult to see.
j and your bones.
k wings.
l survive in their environment.

B **Read and circle *True* or *False*.**

1   If you approach something, you run away from it.   True   False
2 Camouflage helps animals to hide from predators.   True   False
3 Bugs, deer, and fish are examples of creatures.   True   False
4 Predators are eaten by prey.   True   False
5 A sudden change happens slowly.   True   False
6 You should watch out for cars when crossing the street.   True   False

C **Read and complete the paragraph.**

flesh   approach   watch out   sudden   prey   camouflage   evolve   creatures

The ocean is a dangerous place, and most of the [1] _____________ that live there have to [2] _____________ for [3] _____________ attacks by predators. Over thousands of years, prey species [4] _____________ in different ways to avoid becoming food. Crabs, for example, have a hard shell that protects their [5] _____________ from the bites of most predators. But for some crabs, that's not enough. A group called decorator crabs stick plants and other animals on their shells as [6] _____________ . Their body shape is hidden by all of the decorations. If predators [7] _____________ , they don't usually notice that the crabs are there, so the crabs avoid becoming [8] _____________ .

A Complete the sentences.

> settings   intentions   gullible   cautious   private   filter

1 If you believe someone who tells you that the moon is made of cheese, you're being _______________ .

2 If you look several times in both directions before you cross the road, you're being _______________ .

3 If you don't have permission, you can't enter someone's living room, because it's _______________ .

4 If you want to change how something looks in a photo, you can use a _______________ .

5 If you don't like the sounds that a phone makes, you can change the _______________ .

6 If you cause a problem, people will be less upset with you if you had good _______________ .

B Read and circle the correct option.

1 **A:** Do you think I can trust this website to keep my information **private** / **gullible**? I don't want everyone on the Internet to have access to it!

   B: I don't know. But you're probably right to be **filter** / **cautious**.

2 **A:** I took this photo on Mom's phone, but it's too dark. Maybe I should take it again using different **intentions** / **settings**.

   B: Maybe. And if that doesn't work, you could download an app that has **filters** / **cautious** to make photos brighter.

3 **A:** The man on the phone said he was from the computer company. I didn't know his **intention** / **setting** was to figure out Mom and Dad's passwords!

   B: Oh dear! You need to be less **private** / **gullible** when people call.

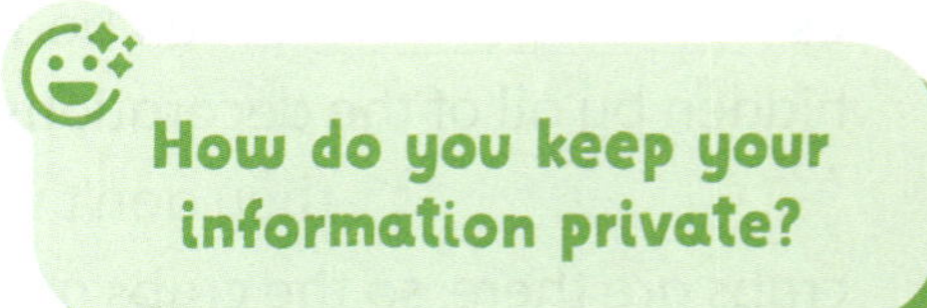

A Read the instructional guide. Label the different sections.

Title   Numbered instructions   Introduction

____

____

____

How to Protect a Device from Malware

If there's malware on your device, it can allow people to find out private information about you, show you advertisements that you don't want to see, and spread malware to your friends. Follow these instructions to keep your device secure and protect it from these threats.

1 Recognize signs of malware on your device. For example, your device might suddenly get slower, be impossible to turn off, or keep crashing. There might be surprising new software icons, messages or advertisments on the screen. Or your friends might say that you sent them a weird message.

2 If you suspect that there is malware on your device, stop doing anything with the device that requires private information such as passwords.

3 Get your parents' permission to download some software to protect against malware, if you don't already have it. Use the software to find and delete malware on your device.

4 In future, avoid doing things that might get malware on your device. Be cautious about downloading free stuff such as movies or games, and about using links to websites in advertisements and messages.

B Answer the questions.

1 Why is the title useful to the reader?

____

2 What is the purpose of the introduction?

____

3 How does the writer organize the instructions?

____

4 Who do you think the writer expects to read the guide?

____

C You're going to write an instructional guide. Brainstorm. Write your ideas in the graphic organizer below.

D Outline your best idea by completing the chart.

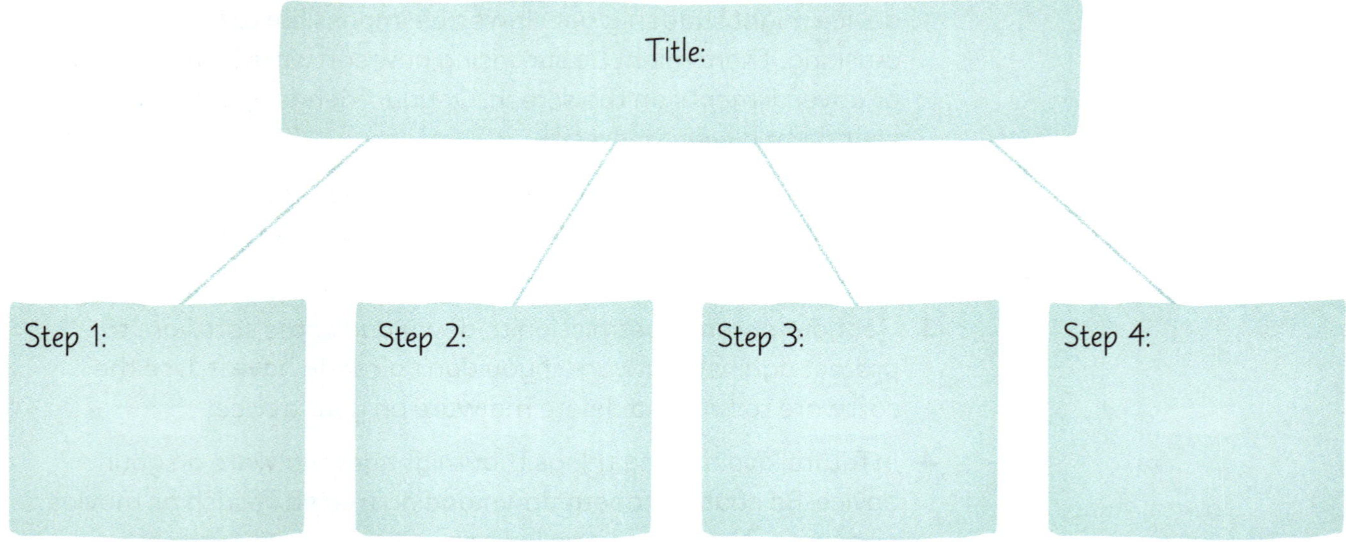

E Now write the first draft of your instructional guide in your notebook. 

- Use a title that explains the content of your instructional guide.
- Use your introduction to explain why people should do what you say.
- Number your instructions.
- Address the people who will be doing the thing that you describe.

F Check your work and make any necessary changes.

- Did you do everything in the list in **E**?
- Is your grammar, spelling, and punctuation correct?
- Is your writing clear and easy for other people to understand?

G Now write the final draft of your instructional guide in your notebook. 

A **Read and circle the correct option.**

1 It wasn't our **malware** / **intention** / **flesh** to buy something today. But there were some great **counterfeits** / **settings** / **bargains** in the stores, so it seemed a good idea.

2 There was a **sudden** / **genuine** / **private** noise as a stone hit the car window, and then the glass **deleted** / **trusted** / **shattered** into hundreds of pieces.

3 If you think the boy in that photo genuinely looks like that, you're very **secure** / **cautious** / **gullible**. He's clearly used a **filter** / **suspect** / **damage**!

B **Unscramble the words to complete the paragraph.**

It's not surprising that snakes have a scary [1] r_____________ (atretiuopn), because their bites can be very dangerous. Some snakes have [2] c_____________ (aflmoeuacg) that makes them difficult to see. Others have bright color patterns that warn other [3] c_____________ (tusrceare) that they are dangerous. Some snakes aren't dangerous, but they use imitation to stay safe. They have [4] e_____________ (levedov) with the same color patterns as the dangerous snakes. Predators don't [5] a_____________ (paprcoah) them because they think they are too dangerous to be their [6] p_____________ (epyr).

C **Read and complete the paragraph with the future continuous form of the verbs in parentheses.**

I can't wait for next Tuesday, because my class [1] _____________________________ (not study) in our classroom. We [2] _____________________________ (visit) a nature reserve! At nine o'clock, I [3] _____________________________ (sit) on the bus next to my best friend Arthur. At ten o'clock, we [4] _____________________________ (explore) the reserve, and an expert [5] _____________________________ (teach) us about the animals there. And at one o'clock, we [6] _____________________________ (have) a picnic lunch. Will the animals at the reserve [7] _____________________________ (try) to eat our food? I hope not!

Think and Reflect: Unit 3

My understanding of imitation ☆☆☆☆☆

How well I achieved my goal for Unit 3 ☆☆☆☆☆

The most interesting thing that I learned _____________________________________

My goal for Unit 4 _____________________________________

4 Why do living things need a good sense of balance?

A Complete the sentences.

> gravity   base   upright   tube   blurry   evidence

1 The ______________ of a tree trunk is always wider than it is at the top.

2 When Tom isn't wearing his glasses, everything looks ______________ to him.

3 Apples fall to the ground because ______________ pulls them toward the Earth.

4 The boat struggled to stay ______________ because of the storm.

5 The scientists quickly found ______________ that dinosaurs had lived here.

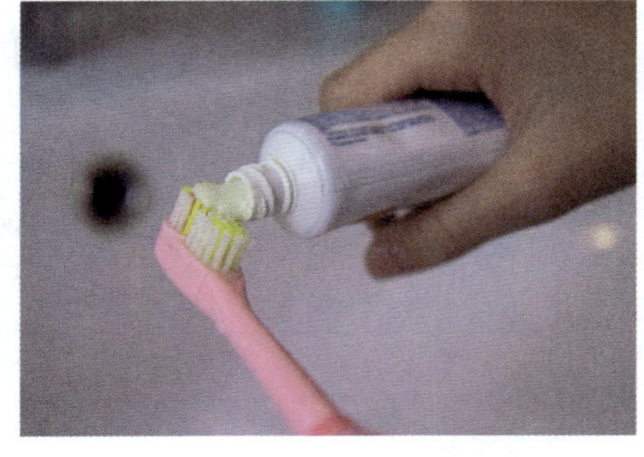

6 It isn't possible to get toothpaste back into its ______________!

B Match to make sentences.

1 Dogs are sometimes trained to detect …   a ear.

2 That bottle won't fall over …   b so that you can get into the back.

3 It's not possible to see your own inner …   c in his fingers.

4 The front seats of this car tilt …   d because it has a wide base.

5 The ladder isn't stable …   e so you shouldn't climb it.

6 My dad has a problem with the joints …   f diseases using their sense of smell.

A Complete the sentences with the noun form of these adjectives. Use the suffix *-ness*.

~~happy~~   kind   weak   dark   ill   aware   lonely   dizzy

1   ___Happiness___ makes people laugh and smile.

2   Jin couldn't grip the branch of the tree because of the ________________ in her hand.

3   Taking care of your friend when they don't feel well at school is an example of ________________.

4   It's good to spend time with friends and family to avoid a feeling of ________________.

5   There was a power outage and we couldn't see anything in the ________________.

6   The students worked hard to raise ________________ of the trash problems on the beach.

7   Sneezing and coughing are signs you have an ________________.

8   If you run around in circles for a long time, you'll experience ________________.

B Underline the defining relative clause in each sentence. Circle the noun that it describes.

1   A carpenter is a (person) who makes things from wood.

2   Poets are writers who create poems.

3   Bananas are fruits that have yellow peel.

4   Is that the boy who doesn't like chocolate?

5   A coder is someone who can write computer programs.

6   A panda is an animal that is endangered.

C Write sentences using *who*, *that*, or *which*.

1 My aunt is the person	who	was in that movie?
2 Which man is the builder		is incredibly tall.
3 What's the name of the actor	that	we need to call?
4 A skyscraper is a building		doesn't like dessert.
5 I don't know anybody	which	lost her purse.
6 What is the number		built those houses?

1   ____

2   ____

3   ____

4   ____

5   ____

6   ____

 Check (✓) the sentences that use defining relative pronouns correctly. Write the correct word for the sentences that don't.

1 ☐ A parent is somebody that has a child. ___________

2 ☐ This smartphone is a device who is very useful. ___________

3 ☐ Miss Nasreen is the teacher that taught me to read music. ___________

4 ☐ These are the friends which I want to invite to my party. ___________

5 ☐ There's the hospital which I was born in! ___________

 Unscramble the sentences.

1 are / who / Soccer players and tennis players / people / play sports

____

2 eats prey / is / an animal / A predator / that

____

3 Listening to music / I / enjoy / that / is / an activity

____

4 which / devices / Tablets and smartphones / are / useful / are

____

 Complete the sentences with defining relative clauses and the words in parentheses.

1 A vet is a person

_______________________________ .

(take care / animals)

2 A digger is a machine

_______________________________ .

(dig / holes)

3 A baseball player is an athlete

_______________________________ .

(use / a bat)

4 A cold is an illness

_______________________________ .

(cause / coughs and sneezes)

5 A train is a vehicle

_______________________________ .

(carry / people)

6 A paramedic is a person

_______________________________ .

(drive / an ambulance)

What is a hobby that you enjoy?

A **Read the science magazine article. When do babies learn to walk?**

Animals or Babies Which Walk First?

This zebra is just a few hours old. Twenty minutes after it was born, it stood up. An hour or two later, it could walk and run!

Similarly, this lamb started walking about a day after it was born. Its legs are a little wobbly and it falls over a lot, but if it needs to it can walk and run.

Animals like horses, elephants, and sheep can stand, walk, and run soon after they're born because they have a high percentage of bone and muscle. This makes them strong. Their brains are fully developed, too, so they can start learning from the adult animals immediately. And four-legged animals are pretty stable when they walk because their four legs make a large base of support, and their center of gravity isn't very high. Running on four legs is efficient – animals can run long distances quickly. But why do they need to be able to walk and run so soon? It's to help them escape from predators! If they detect a predator nearby, they don't want to be its next meal, so they have to be able to run away – fast!

Have you ever wondered why human babies can't immediately stand upright and begin walking?

Human babies take between 9 and 18 months to walk. That's because we develop in a different way from mammals like elephants and sheep. When we're born, we have a lot of fat, our bones are soft, and many of our joints are separated from each other. We also have large heads because we have big brains. The combination of these things makes it challenging for us to carry our own weight and maintain balance. There's another problem, too. Unlike many animals, we aren't born with fully developed brains. In fact, our brains aren't fully developed until we're about 25 years old, so we have to learn things as we grow. Before we can walk, we need to learn to control our legs, keep our balance, stand up, and move our weight from one leg to the other without falling over!

Do you know why humans walk on two legs, not four?

Scientists have many theories about this, but the most popular theory is that walking on two legs requires less energy. Also, using two legs means that our arms and hands are free to carry things, so it makes us more efficient.

What do you think?

B **Underline these words in the text.**

stable   joints   falls over   base   upright   detect   gravity

C **Circle the correct option.**

1 A baby zebra can walk when it is a few **months** / **hours** old.

2 Lambs can walk and run about a **day** / **year** after they're born.

3 Many mammals **have** / **don't have** fully developed brains when they're born.

4 Some animals need to walk and run immediately because of their **parents** / **predators**.

5 Human babies take up to 18 **months** / **weeks** to walk.

6 Human brains take up to 25 **years** / **months** to fully develop.

D **Read the article again. Paraphrase the paragraph about human babies.**

____

____

____

____

____

____

A **Circle the correct option.**

1 Marathon running is a sport that needs a lot of **core** / **endurance**.

2 When you play sports, try not to **get injured** / **tackle**.

3 The basketball player jumped into **mid-air** / **distance**.

4 A hundred meters is a short **distance** / **pace** to run.

5 When I hike, I like to walk at my own **core** / **pace**.

6 I've never played **rugby** / **tackle**. Have you?

7 Soccer players **tackle** / **pace** each other to get the ball.

8 My brother is doing exercises to make his **mid-air** / **core** strong.

B **Read and circle *True* or *False*.**

1	Ocean rowing is an endurance sport.	**True**	**False**
2	If you get injured, it never hurts.	**True**	**False**
3	Everyone learns new things at a different pace.	**True**	**False**
4	Rugby is a type of music.	**True**	**False**
5	A football player might tackle somebody during a game.	**True**	**False**
6	A distance can be long or short.	**True**	**False**
7	It's impossible to throw a ball into mid-air.	**True**	**False**
8	The muscles around your lower back and stomach are your core.	**True**	**False**

C **Read and complete the paragraph.**

core   rugby   pace   injured   distance

I'm on my school's [1]______________ team. It's my favorite sport. Before practice, we usually go for a run. I used to run only 200 meters before I got tired. I got upset that I wasn't very fast. However, my coach told me to not give up! She told me to run at my own [2]______________. Now I can run for a much longer [3]______________ before I get tired. During practice, we do exercises that help keep our [4]______________ strong. We have our second match next weekend. I missed the first match because I was [5]______________. I'm so excited to finally be able to play in a match!

A **Check (✓) the correct option.**

1 This owl's head turns easily. It can … its neck a long way.

☐ look out for   ☐ twist

2 I love animals so I want to be a … when I grow up.

☐ risky   ☐ zoologist

3 There are many species of fish … the surface of our oceans.

☐ beneath   ☐ otherwise

4 I'd like to touch that snake, but it's too … .

☐ twist   ☐ risky

5 Stop running in circles, … you'll get dizzy.

☐ otherwise   ☐ beneath

6 We need to … bears when we go hiking in the mountains.

☐ twist   ☐ look out for

B **Read and complete the dialogue.**

risky   otherwise   zoologist   beneath   twist   look out

Nicki: Hey, Marc. Slow down! Dad told us to [1] ______________ for bugs.

Marc: Oh no, Nicki! I saw something moving!

Nicki: What? Really? Where? I hope you're joking, [2] ______________ I'm going to get scared.

Marc: I'm not joking. There's a huge bug just [3] ______________ the rock. It might be an enormous spider.

Nicki: Which rock? This one next to me? Oh! Wow! Look! It has six long legs. That's not a spider. What do you think it is?

Marc: I've no idea. I'm not a [4] ______________ ! Should we catch it and ask Dad?

Nicki: No, that's too [5] ______________ . It might sting or bite us. Let's leave it alone.

Marc: I just saw it [6] ______________ its whole body. It's looking at us! Run!

Nicki: You're not funny, Marc!

Writing Study

A **Check (✓) the sentences that use a connector to show comparison. Underline the connectors.**

1 ☐ Like horses, zebras can stand upright soon after they're born.

2 ☐ Babies can't stand upright and they cry a lot.

3 ☐ Some monkeys walk on two legs, just as humans do.

4 ☐ Monkeys can't walk on two legs for very long.

5 ☐ Good balance is important for walking. Similarly, running requires good balance.

B **Rewrite these sentences using the connectors in parentheses.**

1 Squirrels and birds both live in trees. (just as)

Squirrels live in trees, just as birds do.

2 Many land animals need protection. Many ocean animals also need protection. (similarly)

3 Marathon running is an endurance sport. Ocean-rowing is an endurance sport. (like)

4 Sportspeople are athletes. Dancers are, too. (just as)

5 I enjoy math and so does my brother. (like)

C **Write a paragraph to describe an animal you like. Use connectors to make comparisons.**

Like my dad, I really enjoy the natural world. All animals are fascinating, just as plants are, but the chimpanzee is the animal that I find most interesting. Chimpanzees often walk on two legs, like us! I love watching chimpanzees playing. Similarly, I like watching them when they're learning something new. Last month, I saw a documentary about chimpanzees in the wild. They were enjoying eating bananas, just as I do!

A **Unscramble the words to complete the paragraph.**

I'm an eager sports player. I enjoy playing [1] r______________ (b y g u r), even though
I [2] f______________ ______________ (l l a f e v o r) in the dirt a lot! It's fun to
[3] t______________ (k c l e a t) other players for the ball. My coach says I need to do
exercises to make my [4] c______________ (r o c e) strong so that I don't [5] g______________
______________ (e t g i d j u r e n) while I'm playing.

B **Match the words to their definitions.**

1 endurance ●		● **a**	the opposite of outer
2 distance ●		● **b**	a person who studies animals
3 inner ●		● **c**	the opposite of safe
4 blurry ●		● **d**	the length between two points
5 twist ●		● **e**	the ability to do something hard for a long time
6 zoologist ●		● **f**	turn something
7 beneath ●		● **g**	not clear
8 risky ●		● **h**	at a lower level

C **Circle the correct option.**

1 A saw is a tool **that** / **who** cuts wood.
2 Is this the teacher **which** / **who** lent you the book?
3 There's the building **who** / **that** is one hundred years old.
4 A dictionary is a book **that** / **who** gives the meanings of words.
5 Let's go to the store **which** / **who** your mom works in.
6 Which is the bike **who** / **that** you like – the green one or the silver one?

Think and Reflect: Unit 4

My understanding of balance ☆☆☆☆☆

How well I achieved my goal for Unit 4 ☆☆☆☆☆

The most interesting thing that I learned ______________________________________

My goal for Unit 5 ______________________________________

5 What can happen when we have a better balance in our lives?

Vocabulary 1

A Complete the sentences.

varied   awaken   disapproving   hut   remind   bandage

1 There was a small ______________ on the beach.

2 The doctor put a ______________ on my arm.

3 There was a ______________ choice of drinks.

4 I need an alarm clock to ______________ me in the morning.

5 The teacher gave Maria a ______________ look for arriving late.

6 To ______________ us about appointments, Dad puts notes on the refrigerator.

B Match to make sentences.

1 People might say you're clumsy if you …	**a** long run.
2 In a tropical place, there might be a …	**b** bathroom.
3 I would probably be glad if I got a …	**c** fall over.
4 I would probably feel worn out after a …	**d** rainforest.
5 In the interior of a home, there's often a …	**e** math calculation.
6 It was a really complicated …	**f** compliment.

A **Complete the sentences.**

> knowledgeable   affordable   miserable   acceptable   drinkable   breakable

1 That water won't make you ill. It's ____________________ .

2 Our walk was very long, cold, and wet. We were ____________________ .

3 I don't have enough money to buy that. It's just not ____________________ .

4 She seems to be an expert in everything! She's so ____________________ .

5 Be careful not to drop the bottle. It's made of glass, so it's ____________________ .

6 There's a school uniform, so wearing other clothes at school isn't ____________________ .

B **Underline the defining relative clause in each sentence. Circle the noun that it describes.**

1 That's the girl whose name I couldn't remember.

2 This is the beach where we went swimming yesterday.

3 That isn't the hospital where my aunt works.

4 Is Leo the boy whose brother goes to your dance class?

5 That's the building where Imdad lives.

6 It's Defne whose book I lost.

C **Circle the correct option.**

1 There were comfortable beds in the treehouse **that** / **where** we slept.

2 The treehouse was near the beach **that** / **where** we noticed from the boat.

3 There were monkeys **that** / **whose** noises awakened us every morning.

4 There were people in the group **that** / **whose** skills helped us to survive.

5 Every day, we went to places **that** / **where** berries and coconuts grew.

6 It was my mom **that** / **whose** caught the biggest fish.

7 There wasn't a kitchen **that** / **where** we could cook.

8 I was the person **that** / **whose** did most of the cooking.

D **Join the sentences using defining relative clauses with _where_ or _whose_.**

1 That's the school. My brother studies there.

  <u>That's the school where my brother studies.</u>

2 Melissa is my friend. Her sister was in a TV show.

  ____

3 This is the hut. We keep our stuff for the beach there.

  ____

4 That's the tree. Its fruit tasted so delicious.

  ____

5 Mr. Marielos is the teacher. His math classes really helped me.

  ____

6 We couldn't find the place. People play beach volleyball there.

  ____

E **Unscramble the words in parentheses to complete the sentences.**

1 That's the teacher ________________________________ . (my dentist / whose / husband / is)

2 It was ________________________________ . (were / my mom / jokes / the funniest / whose)

3 I love ________________________________ . (ate / where / the restaurant / we)

4 Don't swim ________________________________ . (where / at beaches / are / no lifeguards / there)

5 I met ________________________________ . (someone / grandmother / an astronaut / whose / was)

6 They visited ________________________________ . (we / where / stayed / the town / last summer)

F **Complete the defining relative clauses using _where_, _whose_, or _that_ and the words in parentheses.**

1 He's the cameraman <u>whose camera was broken</u> . (camera / was broken)

2 That's the rock pool ________________________________ . (I / caught / a fish)

3 She's the woman ________________________________ . (built / the hut)

4 I saw a boy ________________________________ . (arm / bandaged)

5 Let's relax somewhere ________________________________ .
  (it / isn't / too hot)

6 I like the girl ________________________________ .
  (family / is / from the Philippines)

A Read the feature article. How does Callum feel now about his decision to perform in a Broadway musical?

Life on Broadway: A Child Star Tells All

We love to see talented children performing in movies or on stage. But have you ever wondered what it would be like to be one of them? Callum O'Malley tells us all about it.

I loved singing, dancing, and acting when I was young. When my drama teacher told me that a child performer was needed for a musical, I was really eager to get the part. It was on Broadway, the area of New York where all the most famous theaters are! I went to the theater where the musical was on, and the people in charge of it asked me to perform a few songs for them. Six weeks later I had a part in the show. I was only nine, and I was so excited!

I performed six evenings a week, and I did two afternoon performances, too. I enjoyed it at first. It was a cool challenge to perform as well as possible every night, and a great feeling when the audience clapped. The adult performers were really good fun, and told me amazing stories about their experiences in the theater.

However, I was spending more time with the other performers than with my family and friends. I had to stay up late for the show and then get up early for school the next morning. I often fell asleep in the car on my way home, but sometimes I still had to finish my homework when I got back. Before long I was worn out. I started to feel envious of people whose lives were less complicated than mine.

I gave it all up when I was eleven. Some of the people at the theater were a little disapproving, but it felt great to have a more varied life again. I didn't stop performing altogether – I took part in school plays and dance performances. But I could also play basketball, and cook, and spend time with my friends. And I had more energy for my studies, so I started to do better at school, too.

These days, hearing tunes from the musical always reminds me of that time in my life: singing on stage in a pool of light, with a thousand people watching me. I feel proud of my achievement, and I'm glad that I had the opportunity. Now that I'm studying engineering in college, I don't have time for drama. But I sometimes wonder if I might return to the stage one day. Who knows!

B **Underline these words in the text.**

worn out   varied   glad   complicated   reminds   disapproving

C **Read and write *True* or *False*.**

1 Callum was a talented child.

2 Callum got a part in a musical on Broadway.

3 Callum left school so that he could work in the theater.

4 Callum stopped working in the theater because someone better was chosen for his part.

5 Callum realized that the decision he made when he was eleven was a mistake.

6 These days, Callum never performs on stage.

D **What do you think? Use inference to answer the questions.**

1 Did Callum do well when he first went to the theater to perform songs for the people in charge of the musical?

2 Was Callum happy that he was spending so much time with the other performers?

3 When he was performing on Broadway, did Callum do as well at school as he did before and afterward?

4 Does Callum like cooking?

5 Does Callum want to be a performer as an adult?

A **Read and complete the advertisement.**

solos   talent   value   gigs   set up   lead singer   drum kit   unappreciated

Do You Want To Be in a Band?

We **1** _______________ our rock band Wednesday Wolves last year. We **2** _______________ cooperation, and we work together to create new songs and sounds. We have a **3** _______________ and all the other equipment that we need, and we've performed a lot of **4** _______________. But we now need a new **5** _______________ – someone with a great voice and a lot of musical **6** _______________. Perhaps you've sung **7** _______________ in school performances, or perhaps you just sing in the shower. If you feel that your voice is **8** _______________ and needs a wider audience, get in touch! We can give you the opportunity to perform regularly.

B **Circle the correct option.**

1 She feels unappreciated because she thinks
   everyone / **no one** notices her hard work.

2 She wants a drum kit because
   she likes playing **loud** / **quiet** instruments.

3 She doesn't want to do a solo because
   she prefers performing **in a group** / **alone**.

4 She's the lead singer in the band because she
   is shy / **has the best voice**.

5 She went to a gig because she wanted to **hear her favorite band** / **buy a new keyboard**.

6 People think she has artistic talent because **she doesn't like to paint** /
   her pictures are really beautiful.

A **Read and circle *True* or *False*.**

1 A sense of belonging makes you feel lonely. **True** **False**

2 You congratulate someone if they achieve something good. **True** **False**

3 You should rely on people who never do the things that they promise. **True** **False**

4 When you're hanging out with friends, you have something important to do together. **True** **False**

5 You can contribute to something with your money or your hard work. **True** **False**

6 If you divide something equally between two people, each person gets exactly half of it. **True** **False**

B **Read and complete the dialogue.**

> belonging   contribute   hang out   congratulate   rely   equally

Blanca: Hey, Jorge, I wanted to [1] ________________ you! You have a part in the school play!

Jorge: Really? That's so cool! It gives me a real sense of [2] ________________ when everyone's preparing for a performance together. Are you in it, too?

Blanca: Not as an actor, but I'm going to [3] ________________ in another way. I'll be helping with the lights.

Jorge: That's fantastic, Blanca! I think the lights and the acting are [4] ________________ important.

Blanca: Me too. It wouldn't be a great play if the audience couldn't see the stage! The actors really [5] ________________ on the people who do the lights.

Jorge: That's so true! And if we're both involved in the play, maybe we'll have time to [6] ________________ together more. I can't wait!

A **Complete the sentences with these reflexive pronouns.**

> yourselves   myself   herself   themselves   yourself   itself

1 Did you hurt ________________ when you fell, Stanley?

2 Your bedroom won't clean ________________ , you know, Zainab!

3 I hope you enjoyed ________________ at the party, everyone.

4 They felt very proud of ________________ for winning the competition.

5 I sometimes talk to ________________ when I'm alone.

6 Aurelia played her drum kit so loudly that she gave ________________ a headache.

B **Check (✓) the sentences that use a reflexive pronoun correctly. Write the correct word for the sentences that don't.**

1 ☐ I sent themselves a message, but they didn't get it.   ____them____

2 ☐ He looked at himself in the mirror.   ________________

3 ☐ We bought ourselves some delicious ice cream.   ________________

4 ☐ The cat washes itself every morning.   ________________

5 ☐ My sister helped myself to come up with some ideas.   ________________

C **Write a paragraph about how you and your family take care of yourselves. Use reflexive pronouns.**

I take care of myself by eating a lot of vegetables and whole grains. I also try to give myself enough sleep every night, but that's not easy because my alarm clock awakens me very early in the morning. My brother and I keep ourselves in shape by playing on the trampoline in our yard. My brother challenges himself to do difficult jumping routines, and I try to copy him. My mom keeps herself in good shape by doing dance routines in the living room.

____

____

____

____

____

A Unscramble the words to complete the paragraphs.

1 I hope you sing a s_____________ (o l s o) in the school concert.
   You have a lot of t_____________ (n l t a e t) as a singer.

2 Yesterday, I walked into a lamppost and cut my head. It was so
   c_____________ (s l u c y m) of me! My head has a big white
   b_____________ (a g b d e a n) on it now, and it really hurts.

3 Tomorrow is going to be a c_____________ (e d i c o l a t m c p)
   day. We have appointments in three different places in the morning,
   and we have to r_____________ (y r l e) on buses to get us there.

4 My teacher gave me a d_____________ (d s i p a v p o r n i g) look
   because I arrived late to class. I told her I missed the bus because I was
   w_____________ _____________ (o r w n t o u). I need to go to bed early tonight!

B Read and circle the correct option.

I live in a [1] **glad** / **worn out** / **tropical** country, so it's hot all year. I [2] **value** / **awaken** / **remind** electric fans more than anything else in my home. They're better for the environment than air conditioning. And if you [3] **contribute them** / **hang them out** / **set them up** correctly, they keep the [4] **gig** / **interior** / **drum kit** of the house nice and cool. In my opinion, they are an [5] **disapproving** / **unappreciated** / **varied** appliance!

C Complete the sentences with the pronouns *where*, *whose*, or *that*.

1 I want to have a vacation in a place _____________ I can go snorkeling.

2 I want friends _____________ care about me as much as I care about them.

3 There's someone in my class _____________ hobby is to make bags from old jeans.

4 You'll be happier if you have friendships _____________ are balanced.

5 What's the name of the club _____________ you met your friend Victor?

6 Who was that girl _____________ solo was so amazing?

Think and Reflect: Unit 5

My understanding of balance ☆☆☆☆☆

How well I achieved my goal for Unit 5 ☆☆☆☆☆

The most interesting thing that I learned _________________________________

My goal for Unit 6 _________________________________

6 How can we get a more balanced understanding of something?

A Complete the sentences.

howl   precious   encounter   loyal   conservation   playful

1 These monkeys are ________________ .

2 These diamonds are ________________ .

3 Have you ever heard a wolf's ________________ ?

4 This park is for the ________________ of sea turtles.

5 Dogs are usually very ________________ to their owners. They love them for ever.

6 I don't think I ever want to ________________ a rattlesnake!

B Match to make sentences.

1 I don't like that man because he is … to animals. •

2 … the terrible traffic jam, we arrived on time. •

3 …, I will get good grades on my tests this year. •

4 The foxes in our area … the chickens on the farms. •

5 There's a good … of clean water in the mountains for us to drink. •

6 My family is going to … a child, so I'm getting a new sister! •

• **a** Despite

• **b** threaten

• **c** adopt

• **d** cruel

• **e** Hopefully

• **f** supply

A Complete the sentences with the prefix *mis-* or *re-*.

1 I _______ spelled the word "serendipity" because it was a new word for me.

2 It's going to rain tomorrow. We need to _______ think our beach plans.

3 Grandma's cat was missing for a week. Then it _______ appeared in her kitchen!

4 There's one student in my class who sometimes _______ behaves.

5 Let's go and _______ fill our water bottles. I'm thirsty!

6 Nobody likes people who _______ treat others. It's unkind.

7 Don't throw that paper away. We can _______ use it to draw on.

8 My friend got upset with me because she _______ understood what I said.

B Underline the nondefining relative clause in each sentence.

1 Brussels, which is the capital of Belgium, is famous for its chocolates.

2 Martina, who is in sixth grade, is the best actress in our school.

3 Wolves, which are very rare in my country, are fascinating animals.

4 The Empire State Building, which is in New York, was built in 410 days!

5 Mr. Lukas, who is a teacher, spoke to the students.

6 Cricket, which is popular in some countries, is a sport I'd like to try.

7 This phone, which belonged to my dad, looks very old-fashioned.

8 Fast food usually has a lot of salt and sugar, which aren't good for your health.

C Check (✓) the sentences that use nondefining relative clauses.

1 ☐ Spinach is a vegetable that I like eating.

2 ☐ Is this the book that you wanted to read?

3 ☐ I ride the subway every day with my mom, who works in the city.

4 ☐ Quaggas are animals that became extinct a long time ago.

5 ☐ Dodos, which were a type of bird, died out at the end of the 17th century.

6 ☐ My favorite music, which is hip hop, is very popular.

7 ☐ Are these the gloves that you're looking for?

8 ☐ Ben's uncle, who lives in Ontario, is a doctor.

1 This person, who …

2 This type of transportation, which …

3 This living thing, which …

4 This word, which …

a lives in Asia and Africa, is very heavy.

b is a synonym of amusing, often describes a joke.

c is very fast, is used by many people.

d works in a restaurant, prepares meals.

e funny

f a bullet train

g a chef

h an elephant

E Complete the sentences with *who* or *which*.

1 Pietro, _______________ is my best friend, video called me on the weekend.

2 Larisa, _______________ is part of a rock band, is a great singer.

3 Astronomy, _______________ is the study of the universe, is absolutely fascinating.

4 Miss Kimpa, _______________ is our class teacher, can sing and dance better than anyone I know.

5 This national park, _______________ is famous around the world, is my favorite place to visit.

6 Tardigrades, _______________ are tiny animals, can survive in many extreme environments.

F Read the two sentences. Rewrite them as one sentence using nondefining relative clauses.

1 İstanbul is an interesting, exciting place. It's Türkiye's largest city.

İstanbul, which is Türkiye's largest city, is an interesting, exciting place.

2 Popcorn was invented in the 1880s. All my friends like it.

____

3 My great-grandmother is 85. She goes swimming every day.

____

4 Ornithology is the study of birds. I think it's interesting.

____

A Read the story. Look at the pictures in the story and make a prediction. What will Eli learn?

Please Don't Squash Us!

"Help!" shouted Eli.

Her brother, Tonio, ran to find out what was wrong.

"Are you hurt, Eli?" he asked.

"There's a bee! Quick, squash it!"

"No! That's cruel. Just walk away, Eli," replied Tonio. "It isn't threatening you."

"It is! It's going to sting me!" Eli let out a howl like a frightened animal.

"What's going on?" asked Carlos, the park gardener.

"It's Eli. She's scared of the bee," said Tonio. "Hopefully, it'll fly away soon."

Carlos stepped forward to take a closer look at the bee. "It's a beautiful honeybee," he said, gently. "We need bees in the park. Without bees, there would be no pollination. And without pollination, we wouldn't have plants. And without plants … "

"We'd get hungry!" said Tonio.

Hmm, thought Eli. *I didn't realize that.*

"Come with me," said Carlos. "I'm going to plant roses, and you can help. Let's dig some holes."

As Carlos began to dig, Eli spotted several wiggly earthworms.

"Ewww!" she said. "Slimy, yucky earthworms! Let's catch them and use them for fishing!"

"No way!" said a voice. "Despite what you might think, those earthworms are precious!" Eli looked up and saw Narita, another park gardener.

"How can they be precious?" asked Eli. "They're just disgusting, wiggly things that live in dirt!"

"No, they aren't," replied Narita. "Earthworms are partly responsible for the supply of air and water underground. They make tiny tunnels and that makes it a lot easier for plants to thrive in our farms, parks, and yards."

"Really?" asked Eli.

"Really! But that's not all. Earthworms eat leaves and dead plants. They turn them into compost. As the earthworms wiggle around underground, they spread nutrients through the soil. The nutrients allow new plants to grow. And without new plants …"

"We'd get hungry!" said Tonio.

"Exactly!"

OK, so earthworms look a little yucky to me, but they're really useful, thought Eli.

Eli and Tonio walked back toward their parents. On a tree with bright green leaves, Eli noticed a ladybug*. *I wonder …* she thought.

"Tonio, if bees and worms are useful to plants, are ladybugs, too?"

"Sure they are," Tonio smiled. "Ladybugs eat aphids**. Aphids kill plants. So without ladybugs, plants would die, and …"

"We'd get hungry!" replied Eli, laughing. "I get it now!"

Glossary:
ladybug = a small, round beetle that is usually red with black spots
aphids = small insects that use the juices of plants for food

---

B **Underline these words in the text.**

supply   hopefully   howl   precious   despite   threatening   cruel

C **Check (✓) the correct answer.**

1 What did Eli want her brother to do to the honeybee?

☐ squash it   ☐ catch it

2 Which of these animals in the story are pollinators?

☐ the aphids   ☐ the honeybees

3 What do earthworms eat?

☐ aphids   ☐ leaves and plants

4 Why are ladybugs useful?

☐ they eat aphids   ☐ they look pretty

D **Answer the questions.**

1 Whose perspectives did Eli consider? _______________________

2 Was she aware of these perspectives at the beginning of the story? _______________________

3 When she considered other perspectives, did her thoughts about the bee, the earthworm, and the ladybug change? Why? _______________________

A Match to make sentences.

1 You can be destructive …
2 You can burst a …
3 You can break out of …
4 You tend to …
5 You can make an effort to …
6 You can't see beyond …

a bubble or a balloon.
b when you break something.
c be friendly and helpful.
d a door that is closed.
e a jail.
f have similar interests as your friends.

B Read and complete the dialogue.

inconvenient   tend   previous   effort   beyond

Rafa: Oh no! Not another traffic jam! We're never going to make it to the beach! We're going to be here for hours, maybe days …

Zuri: Don't worry, Rafa. We'll be fine. We got through the ^{1} _______________ traffic jam, so I'm sure we'll get through this one, too. It's a little ^{2} _______________, but let's be patient.

Rafa: I don't feel patient! It's already two-thirty and I'd like to go swimming.

Zuri: I know you ^{3} _______________ to get frustrated in traffic, but look, I can already see ^{4} _______________ the next traffic light. There aren't so many cars there.

Rafa: OK, you're right. I see a traffic officer, too. She's making a big ^{5} _______________ to move the cars along.

A **Circle the correct option.**

1. I love going to our local **spokesperson** / **theme park** because it has a huge roller coaster.

2. My friend is trying to **persuade** / **deal** me to go camping with him. But I'm not sure.

3. We go to see my grandparents **regularly** / **biased**. They only live an hour away.

4. The **deal** / **spokesperson** told us that the movie theater had to close because they weren't making enough of a profit.

5. Let's make a **deal** / **persuade**. You lend me your video game for a week and I'll lend you my guitar.

6. I try to see both sides of an argument because I don't want to be **regularly** / **biased**.

B **Read and complete the dialogue.**

> deal   persuade   biased   regularly   theme park

Sam: I'm trying to [1] ________________ my parents to take us to a [2] ________________ on Saturday, but they haven't agreed yet. Do you have any advice for me?

Mina: Can you make a [3] ________________ with them? That's what I usually do.

Sam: What do you mean?

Mina: Well, you could offer to wash their car [4] ________________ . They'd like that.

Sam: Oh, what a great idea!

Mina: I'm sure it'll work, but maybe I'm [5] ________________ .

A **Read the review. Label the different sections.**

Recommendation   Positive points   Short description
Negative points   Topic sentence

SchoolWorld: A Review

SchoolWorld is an international website for children to share ideas and projects.

From my point of view, SchoolWorld is an excellent resource. It allows students around the world to share topics and information that interest them. I really like the way the website aims to bring students of all ages and from all backgrounds together. It's a safe space that any student can access. It has a simple design that is extremely easy to navigate. It also has a translation feature which translates any text you want to read on the site. It can even translate as you type, so it's very easy to have a discussion with other students. Everyone can understand each other! Another cool feature is the "about" button. You can click on it and learn about other schools that are using the site. My school recently posted a project on SchoolWorld. As soon as we posted our project, we began to get reactions from children in schools as far away as Canada and India!

There are a few things that could be better on the SchoolWorld site, however. In my opinion, it would be an improvement if we could upload bigger files more easily. I'd also like the website to add emojis that we could use when we're commenting.

Overall, I definitely recommend SchoolWorld for any student who is interested in what children in other schools are learning, doing, and thinking about. It's a great way of increasing your knowledge in a fun and friendly environment. You also get to make a lot of new and interesting friends.

B **Answer the questions.**

1 What does the first line of the review tell the reader? _______________________________________

2 What are two positive features of the website? _______________________________________

3 What negative points does the reviewer make? _______________________________________

4 Does the reviewer recommend the website? _______________________________________

C **You're going to write a review. Brainstorm. Write your ideas in the graphic organizer below.**

D **Outline your best idea by completing the chart.**

A review of:

Short description:

Positive points:	Negative points:

Recommendation:

E **Now write the first draft of your review in your notebook.**

- Give a short description of the thing that you are reviewing.
- Describe your own experience of it.
- Include both positive and negative points, in separate paragraphs.
- Use topic sentences to introduce the positive and negative points.
- Finish with your general feeling, and a recommendation.

F **Check your work and make any necessary changes.**

- Did you do everything in the list in **E**?
- Is your grammar, spelling, and punctuation correct?
- Is your writing clear and easy for other people to understand?

G **Now write the final draft of your review in your notebook.**

A **Circle the correct option.**

1 **Getting a flat tire** / **Having fun with friends** / **Eating breakfast at the usual time** can be inconvenient.

2 **An ice cream cone** / **A hurricane** / **A T-shirt** can be destructive.

3 You go to a theme park **to have fun** / **to study marine animals** / **to learn about conservation**.

4 **A good friend** / **A computer** / **A work of art** is always loyal.

B **Match the words to their opposites.**

1 biased   a serious

2 regularly   b kind

3 cruel   c fair

4 playful   d almost never

C **Read the two sentences. Rewrite them as one sentence using nondefining relative clauses.**

1 This band is one of my favorites. It's a new band.

____

2 My cousin is going on vacation. He lives in Guadalajara.

____

3 I found my tablet in my backpack. I thought it was lost.

____

4 This recipe is delicious. We copied it from a TV show.

____

5 Lucy is terrible at looking after her stuff. She left her earbuds on the bus.

____

Think and Reflect: Unit 6

My understanding of balance ☆☆☆☆☆

How well I achieved my goal for Unit 6 ☆☆☆☆☆

The most interesting thing that I learned ____

My goal for Unit 7 ____

7 What can provide opportunities to have fun?

Vocabulary 1

A Complete the sentences.

flashlight   scuba diving   sand dune   ceiling   shore   mask

1 His favorite activity is _______________ .

2 There's a spider hanging from the _______________ .

3 I needed a _______________ to see inside the cave.

4 We climbed up a _______________ .

5 She was wearing a tiger _______________ .

6 I found a chest full of treasure on the _______________ .

B Read and circle the correct option.

When my friend invited me to a day skiing with her family, I wasn't eager to go. I've always dreamed of going [1] **ceiling / scuba diving** in a tropical ocean and then relaxing on the warm [2] **mask / shore** afterward, but doing a sport in the cold and snow didn't sound much fun. I was [3] **convinced / hooked** that I would hate it.

"Cold weather is never a problem," she said. "The only problem is a [4] **lack / slope** of warm clothes, and you can borrow some of mine." I decided I should give it a try.

At first my ski boots felt really [5] **lack / tight** and uncomfortable, but my feet soon got used to them. And when I first started moving down the [6] **tight / slope** on my skis, it was an [7] **awesome / convinced** feeling! I think it would be very easy to get [8] **awesome / hooked** on skiing. It's a fantastic sport!

Word Study and Grammar

A Complete the phrasal verbs in these sentences. Use some of these words twice.

up   across   out   for   on   over   into

1 We were disappointed that we didn't come ________________ any snakes on our walk, but seeing a beautiful anteater really made ________________ ________________ it.

2 I gave ________________ playing soccer last year. I used to enjoy it when I was little, but as I grew ________________, I got bored of it.

3 I've always been ________________ drawing, but recently sewing has taken ________________ as my main interest.

4 I always put ________________ a helmet when I do jumps on my mountain bike, so my head doesn't get injured if I wipe ________________ .

B Match the sentences to their functions.

1 I couldn't ride a bike. •

2 Would you teach me, please? •

3 May I sit here? •

4 Could you take a picture of us? •

5 I'll be able to ski soon. •

6 Could I look at your surfboard, please? •

• **a** asking for permission

• **b** describing ability

• **c** making a request

C Read and circle the correct option.

Tiwa: I'm going rock climbing with my mom on Saturday.

Kayin: That sounds fun! Are you a good climber?

Tiwa: I don't know. We went to a cliff last month, and I [1] **was able to** / **may** climb it pretty easily. But before that, we climbed in a different place, and I just [2] **can't** / **couldn't** get to the top. It was impossible!

Kayin: [3] **Could** / **May** you take me with you some time? I'd love to try it.

Tiwa: Yes, sure! Come on Saturday! You're really strong so you [4] **will be able to** / **could** do it really well. And [5] **would** / **may** I come with you to your grandparents' farm one day and go horseback riding?

Kayin: [6] **May** / **Can** you already ride a horse?

Tiwa: No, I've never done it before. [7] **Can you** / **Were you able to** teach me?

Kayin: Definitely, with Grandma's help. This is going to be so much fun!

D Complete the sentences with these modals.

couldn't   will be able to   can't   would   may

1 _______________________ I use your pen, please?

2 She didn't answer because she _______________________ hear me.

3 They _______________________ play ice hockey next year, when they've learned how to skate.

4 _______________________ you take this message to Mrs. Keshani, please?

5 She _______________________ speak German, but she's good at three other languages.

E Look and write sentences with modals and the words in parentheses.

1 _______________________________________

2 _______________________________________

3 _______________________________________

4 _______________________________________

F Read the situations and think of an idea for each one. Write what you will say.

1 You have a request for your parents.

"<u>Could you please drive me to Salma's house?</u>   "

2 You have a request for a friend.

"_______________________________________"

3 You need your teacher's permission to do something.

"_______________________________________"

A Read the informal interview. What are the main things that Veronica likes to see when she's scuba diving?

Cool Hobbies: Scuba Diving

We love finding out about your exciting hobbies! In this interview, we speak to Veronica from Antigua, and learn about the fun that she has scuba diving.

Could you describe how scuba diving feels?

It's wonderful! You're deep underwater, and the only sound is the soft *whoosh whoosh* as you breathe from the oxygen tank on your back. The mask is tight on your face, and the equipment is heavy, but you feel weightless in the water. It's incredibly calm and peaceful in that blue, watery world. Then, suddenly, you are surrounded by tropical fish, or some beautiful coral comes into view. The bright, varied colors that you come across beneath the surface are stunning.

What else can you see underwater?

Shipwrecks! There have been ships crossing my part of the Caribbean Sea for centuries and, sadly, some of these voyages have ended in disaster. People say there are more than a hundred shipwrecks around our island's shores. It can be sad exploring a shipwreck if you know that people lost their lives in it. But it's exciting, too. A shipwreck is like a time capsule, a door into history. You can see so many clues to a past way of life – the ship's design, its navigation equipment, its furniture. Sometimes you can take a flashlight and go into the cabins where the sailors slept or ate.

Does it damage the ships to be underwater for a long time?

Yes. Both metal and wooden ships become weaker and less stable over time, so you have to be really careful if you go inside them. But it's often their time underwater that makes them so interesting to explore. They aren't just ships. They become their own little ecosystems. Coral loves a shipwreck habitat, so it attaches itself to the ship. And a lot of fish and shellfish love coral, so they make their home on the ship, too. Sometimes, I've seen magnificent turtles swimming through a shipwreck, looking for their next meal.

Have you ever discovered a shipwreck that wasn't known about before?

Not yet. On one dive, we were able to search for objects on the sea floor near a wreck. I found a seventeenth-century key, which is in a museum now. That was pretty awesome! But discovering an ancient shipwreck for the first time would be a dream come true. Maybe I'll be able to do that one day!

Do you have any cool hobbies you would like to share with us? We'd love to hear from you!

B Underline these words in the text.

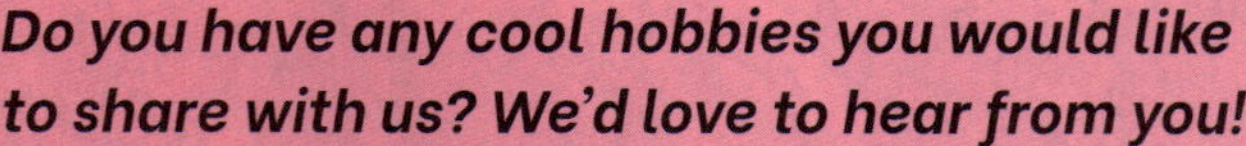

mask   shores   tight   awesome   flashlight   scuba diving

C Think of connections and complete the sentences.

1 **Text to text:** The ideas in this interview remind me of ___________________________________
   (another text) because ___________________________________ .

2 **Text to self:** The ideas in this interview remind me of ___________________________________
   (something in your own life) because ___________________________________ .

3 **Text to world:** The ideas in this interview make me think about ___________________________________
   (something in the world) because ___________________________________ .

D Complete the sentences.

1 When Veronica breathes during scuba diving, she makes a _______________________ sound.

2 Veronica likes the colors that she sees underwater because they are _______________________ .

3 She sometimes feels sad when she's scuba diving if people _______________________ on the ship that she's exploring.

4 She says it's important to be careful inside a shipwreck because, if a ship lies underwater for a long time, it gets _______________________ .

5 A _______________________ that Veronica found is now in a museum.

6 In the future, Veronica would like to be the first person to discover _______________________ .

Would you like to try scuba diving? Why? / Why not?

A   **Read and complete the paragraphs.**

> raindrops   knock over   pings   impressive
> breeze   refreshing   right away   shower

No one expected a storm. First, a gentle [1] _______________ started to blow. Then [2] _______________ began to fall, making little [3] _______________ each time they hit the metal roof of our camper. We didn't suspect [4] _______________ that this was the start of anything more than a quick [5] _______________ .

"How [6] _______________ after this hot weather!" we all said happily. But the rain got heavier, and before long, the wind was howling outside. We were lucky that it didn't [7] _______________ our camper.

It's [8] _______________ that campers are built strong enough to survive that kind of wind!

B   **Match to make sentences.**

1. On a hot day, a cold drink is very …   **a**   right away.
2. Winning an Olympic medal is very …   **b**   shower.
3. It isn't a strong wind; it's just a …   **c**   refreshing.
4. It isn't going to rain all day; it's just a …   **d**   knocked over.
5. Your phone should be silent in the theater, but I heard a …   **e**   raindrops.
6. It's very urgent, so please do it …   **f**   ping.
7. The wind was so strong that our chairs got …   **g**   impressive.
8. I went inside when I started to feel …   **h**   breeze.

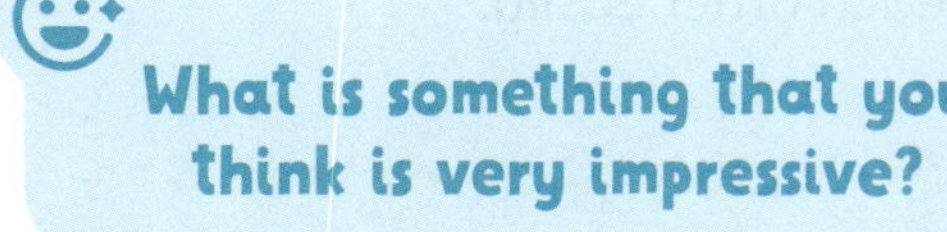

A Check (✓) the correct option.

1 I don't have much money, but I have a few ….

☐ fists   ☐ coins   ☐ knots

2 Make a … with your hand, like this.

☐ fist   ☐ coin   ☐ knot

3 Let's … presents now.

☐ rap   ☐ tie   ☐ exchange

4 My cousin loves listening to ….

☐ knot   ☐ rap   ☐ exchange

5 To play the game, … a scarf over your eyes so you can't see.

☐ rap   ☐ exchange   ☐ tie

6 I have a funny pencil with a … in it.

☐ knot   ☐ fist   ☐ tie

B Complete the sentences.   raps   coins   tie   fists   knots   exchange

1 We'll have to ________________ the rope around the tree trunk.

2 Those little ________________ won't buy much.

3 If you hold up your ________________ people might think you want a fight.

4 We should ________________ phone numbers so we can contact each other easily.

5 I like ________________ that have smart rhymes and word play.

6 There'll be ________________ in your hair if you don't brush it.

A **Look and write the onomatopoeia words.**

whisper   howl   ping   whoosh   splash   boom

1 _______________

2 _______________

3 _______________

4 _______________

5 _______________

6 _______________

B **Match to make sentences.**

1 The stone fell into the lake with a … •   • **a** whisper.

2 You have a message! I heard your cell phone … •   • **b** howl.

3 I don't want anyone to hear, so I have to … •   • **c** ping.

4 The cliff exploded with a loud … •   • **d** splash.

5 During the storm, I listened to the wind … •   • **e** boom.

C **Write a paragraph about your favorite season or weather. Use onomatopoeia.**

My favorite season is the summer. I love to go to the beach and splash in the water to keep cool. But I try to avoid places with big waves that make a booming sound when they hit land. They're scary! There's usually a nice breeze on the shore, and it's a refreshing feeling when it whooshes through my hair. My brother and I like to make a pile of stones and throw shells at it. It's fun when a shell hits the stones with a ping and knocks them over.

____

____

____

____

A **Read and circle the correct option.**

1 While I'm in this desert, I want to take a photo of its famous **sand dunes** / **raps** / **raindrops**. They're very **impressive** / **convinced** / **hooked**!

2 Was that a **fist** / **slope** / **raindrop** that I felt on my face? I hope so! The **flashlight** / **lack** / **ceiling** of rain recently has made the ground really dry.

B **Unscramble the words to complete the sentences.**

It's useful to have:

1 a f______________ (lfhasihtgl) if you want to see in the dark.

2 a b______________ (rezebe) if you want to fly a kite.

3 a s______________ (heorsw) if the plants in the yard need water.

4 some c______________ (nicos) if you want to buy something cheap.

C **Check (✓) the correct options. You can sometimes check more than one.**

1 … I open the window?

☐ Can   ☐ May   ☐ Could

2 She … swim when she was three.

☐ can't   ☐ couldn't   ☐ wasn't able to

3 We … go scuba diving when we're on vacation next month.

☐ will be able to   ☐ couldn't   ☐ would

4 … you drive me to school today, please, Mom?

☐ Can   ☐ May   ☐ Would

5 Dad … run as fast as me because he doesn't do much exercise.

☐ can't   ☐ may   ☐ isn't able to

Think and Reflect: Unit 7

My understanding of fun ☆☆☆☆☆

How well I achieved my goal for Unit 7 ☆☆☆☆☆

The most interesting thing that I learned ____________________________________

My goal for Unit 8 ____________________________________

8 What emotions can we experience when we have fun?

A Complete the sentences.

leak   waterproof   annoyed   exhausted   sink   champion

1 I'm happy that this jacket is ________________ .

2 She won the race! She's the ________________ !

3 He was ________________ after running in the marathon.

4 When did this ship ________________ ?

5 These old bottles both ________________ . I need a new one.

6 Mom is ________________ because I lost her favorite scarf.

B Match to make sentences.

1 We didn't succeed in our project. It was a … .	**a** relieved
2 Having loyal friends and a loving family makes me feel … .	**b** coped
3 Everyone was very … when the swimmer was rescued from the ocean.	**c** failure
4 It was a long and difficult journey, but we all … well.	**d** grateful
5 Our coach asked us to run ten … around the sports field.	**e** suitable
6 We need to wear … clothes to go skiing next weekend.	**f** laps

A Rewrite the sentences, replacing the underlined words with these phrasal verbs. Remember that the object can go in the middle or at the end.

clear up   give away   look forward to   cheer on   come up with   keep at

1 I love to go to my favorite team's soccer games and <u>support</u> them.

<u>I love to go to my favorite team's soccer games and cheer them on.</u>

2 I always <u>get excited about</u> seeing my grandparents.

____

3 The end of the movie is a big surprise. I don't want to <u>reveal</u> it.

____

4 I haven't thought of an idea for my story yet. I still need to <u>think of</u> something.

____

5 My room's a mess, so Dad wants me to <u>clean</u> it.

____

6 I can't speak Quechua very well yet, but if I <u>continue to work at</u> it, I'll improve.

____

B Match the sentences to the situations.

1 That bird may be an owl, but I'm not sure. •

2 Look! There's something that looks like smoke. That must be a volcano, not a regular mountain. •

3 You have to be careful when you cross a busy street. •

4 It could rain tomorrow. Let's take raincoats and umbrellas with us. •

5 That can't be a spider. It only has six legs. •

6 We need to finish our homework before Friday. •

• **a** an obligation

• **b** a possibility

• **c** a deduction

C Circle the correct option.

1 I think skateboarding **needs to** / **may** be even more fun than rollerblading!

2 There **could** / **has to** be a storm tonight. It's very windy.

3 This **can't** / **needs to** be your jacket. It's much too small for you.

4 It was Sunday yesterday, so today **may** / **must** be Monday.

5 The road is blocked. We **will have to** / **might** go a different way.

6 We **have to** / **could** go right away. We're going to be late!

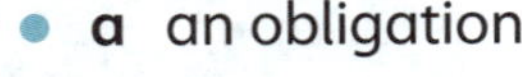

D **Rewrite the sentences with the modal in the correct place.**

1 In the future, most of the games we play be online only. (might)

   ____

2 This game be very popular because it's sold out in our local store. (must)

   ____

3 The rules be very difficult because it's for ages 5 to 14. (can't)

   ____

4 You have two players to play the game. (need to)

   ____

5 A hundred years ago, children play with very simple toys. (had to)

   ____

6 I think we play games with robots one day. (might)

   ____

E **Complete the descriptions with these modals.**

> had to   need to   has to   may   can't   will have to

1 A nurse _______________ look after people who are ill.
2 A frog _______________ be an insect because it has four legs.
3 All plants _______________ have water and light to survive.
4 There are many clouds in the sky, so I think it _______________ rain.
5 I haven't reviewed the words for my spelling test, so tonight I _______________ spend time
   learning them.
6 Before cars were invented, people _______________ walk or bike everywhere.

F **Complete the sentences with a modal.**

1 The school rules say that all students _______________ wear a uniform.
2 That man _______________ be your dad. He's too tall.
3 Great news! Mom says we _______________ go to the movies on the weekend if there's time.
4 I'm not sure, but I think this insect _______________ be a beetle.
5 Everyone is smiling and laughing.
   They _______________ be having a lot of fun!
6 The hike was through a big forest.
   We _______________ plan the route carefully.

> **What do you have to do every day or every week?**

Alegria Vista Celebrates Kermes!

The streets of Alegria Vista came alive this weekend as the community gathered for the annual Mexican kermes festival, a celebration that combines traditional flavors, lively music, and enthusiastic fundraising.

"It was the best kermes so far," said Armando Pilar, a local school teacher who was one of the organizers. "I'm exhausted now, but I'm relieved that it was a success."

"It almost never rains here in Alegria Vista," continued Mercedes Luz, "but on Friday night, people said it might rain! We didn't want our kermes to be a failure, so we found some waterproof clothes and umbrellas just in case. In fact, there was only one short shower on Sunday, and we had a lot of fun!"

From early on Saturday, the smell of *tamales* and *churros* filled the air as our local chefs demonstrated their talent. One of [1] them, Luis Sanchez, made such delicious *tacos de pescado* that a long line formed!

Children and adults enjoyed traditional games, from the popular piñata to ring-throwing competitions. Some people were disappointed to lose, but [2] others were happy to win. The sound of laughter echoed through the city's streets as residents wandered from one stall to [3] another, admiring the work of local artists. There were artworks of all shapes and sizes – paintings, sculptures, clothing, and pottery. We saw many people taking home handmade treasures. From colorful clothes to pretty pots, our artists added an extra layer of cultural variety to the kermes.

At three o'clock, the musicians and dancers came on stage. They performed folk dances as well as pop music suitable for everyone, young and old. This year's entertainment included the Mariachi Children's Academy and DJ Doctor Tunes. As our mayor, Belen Garcia, said, "We're grateful to the musicians. They brought the rich cultural traditions of our country right into our town square."

However, the kermes was more than just a day of celebration. [4] It was also an opportunity for the organizers to raise funds for local schools and community projects. [5] They made this event a powerful force for positive change.

As the sun set, the organizers thanked the community for their support. The success of this year's kermes means that everybody in Alegria Vista is already looking forward to next year's event.

"We're excited to continue the tradition of coming together to celebrate culture and generosity," said [6] the mayor.

B Underline these words in the text.

suitable   relieved   exhausted   waterproof   failure   grateful

C Check (✓) the correct answer.

1 How often does the kermes happen in Alegria Vista?

- [ ] every weekend
- [ ] once a year
- [ ] once a month

2 How often does it rain in Alegria Vista?

- [ ] almost always
- [ ] often
- [ ] almost never

3 Who takes part in the kermes?

- [ ] children and adults
- [ ] only children
- [ ] only artists and chefs

4 What can people buy at the kermes?

- [ ] food and art
- [ ] only clothes
- [ ] music and games

5 What other things can people enjoy doing at the kermes?

- [ ] music, dancing, and games
- [ ] making clothes and pottery
- [ ] cooking tacos

6 What did the organizers work hard to do?

- [ ] clean up the town square
- [ ] raise funds
- [ ] win prizes

D What do the numbered references (1–6) in the local news article refer to? Write.

1 them _______________________

2 others _______________________

3 another _______________________

4 it _______________________

5 they _______________________

6 the mayor _______________________

What community events take place where you live? Do you enjoy them? Why? / Why not?

A **Circle the correct option.**

1 I felt **exhilarated** / **scream** when I rode the roller coaster at the fair.

2 When I feel **powerful** / **tense**, I get a bad feeling in my stomach.

3 **Hormones** / **Tense** like endorphins help me feel less pain.

4 When I want to feel **energized** / **frightened**, I do something that's fun.

5 I'm going to **powerful** / **scream** if you make me touch the beetle.

B **Read and complete the dialogue.**

hormone   frightened   tense   powerful   scream   on purpose   exhilarated

Hayley: Ugh! What's that? I'm scared!

Nuna: What? It's just a little spider. Don't be
1 ________________ . It won't hurt you.
Come closer and take a look.

Hayley: You're trying to scare me
2 ________________ ! You know I don't
like spiders.

Nuna: No, I'm not. It's a fascinating animal.
Look how 3 ________________ it is. It has
tiny legs, but it can run really fast.

Hayley: I'm going to 4 ________________ if it gets
any closer!

Nuna: That's because your body is producing a 5 ________________ that makes you want
to run away from things that scare you. It's called adrenaline! Adrenaline can also
make you feel 6 ________________ . For example, when you do something scary but
fun, like a skateboarding trick!

Hayley: Oh, really? That's interesting.

Nuna: I'll tell you something else that's interesting. Spiders are very cool. They have blue
blood, not red blood like you and I do.

Hayley: Wow! That's amazing.

Nuna: You don't look so 7 ________________ now.

Hayley: Hmm. I guess I'm not. After all, that spider is pretty small and very interesting!

A **Check (✓) the correct option.**

1 The blue team just … the game, but there is still half an hour to play.

   ☐ opposing   ☐ tied

2 The … is big enough for several thousand people to watch the game.

   ☐ shot   ☐ stadium

3 The blues and reds are on … sides.

   ☐ opposing   ☐ ahead

4 The … sent a player off the field for bad behavior.

   ☐ stadium   ☐ referee

5 The red team is … , but they haven't won yet.

   ☐ ahead   ☐ opposing

6 The … landed right inside the goal!

   ☐ tied   ☐ shot

B **Read and circle the correct option.**

Last year, a group of my friends formed their own soccer team, the Fox Strikers. In the summer, they played a game in our city's biggest [1] **stadium** / **referee** , and I went to watch. The Fox Strikers were losing, but they [2] **ahead** / **tied** the game with just a few minutes left to play! It was very exciting! Then, suddenly, one of the Fox Strikers took a powerful [3] **shot** / **tie** and scored a goal. The [4] **opposing** / **stadium** team thought the ball had touched the hand of one of the Fox Strikers, so their goal shouldn't be allowed. But the [5] **referee** / **shot** allowed the goal and the Fox Strikers were [6] **ahead** / **opposing** ! The fans were very tense as they watched the end of the game. But guess what? The Fox Strikers won!

A **Check (✓) the sentences that use alliteration.**

1. ☐ The stunning scenery surprised the students.
2. ☐ My mom is a surgeon at the local hospital.
3. ☐ "Which way?" wondered William.
4. ☐ I thought that my grandparents were away on vacation.
5. ☐ Nobody found the giraffe that escaped from the zoo.
6. ☐ Fiesta Friday is fantastic fun.

B **Match to make sentences with alliteration. Practice saying them aloud.**

1. The terrifying tiger tiptoed …
2. Seven slithery snakes slid …
3. Emilia encouraged Enrico …
4. Bobby bounced his basketball, …
5. Jake's incredible journey through the jungle …

a. silently and softly through the snow.
b. made us jump for joy.
c. breaking the backyard silence.
d. to explore the exciting engine room.
e. toward the tiny turtle.

C **Write a paragraph about a time when you were either frightened or exhilarated. Use alliteration.**

Last summer, I had an exhilarating experience at camp. Our team leaders took us on a hike through a forest. When we reached the middle of the forest, we looked up and saw a zip line! I was seriously scared at first because the zip line was high up in the trees. I decided to be brave and give it a try. As I flew through the air, I felt a fantastic feeling. It was honestly one of the most awesome things I've ever done!

____

____

____

____

A **Complete the sentences.**   grateful   on purpose   annoyed   stadium

1   The city planners are building a new _______________ close to our school! We're all really _______________ because we need somewhere nearby to play our matches.

2   My neighbor was very _______________ when I kicked a ball through his window. Of course I didn't do it _______________, but I can understand why he was so upset.

B **Check (✓) the correct option.**

1   After eating a healthy breakfast, you might feel ….

☐ energized   ☐ opposing

2   Every day of your life, your body produces ….

☐ champions   ☐ hormones

3   If you go to bed very late for several days, you'll feel ….

☐ ahead   ☐ exhausted

4   A boat that has a big hole in the bottom will probably ….

☐ sink   ☐ tie

C **Circle the correct option.**

1   I saw an animal with big ears. It **can't** / **could** be an elephant.

2   I know it **has to** / **can't** be a giraffe because it doesn't have a long neck.

3   It **will have to** / **might** be dangerous, so I won't get close to it.

4   There aren't elephants in my country, so it **must** / **can't** be from the zoo.

5   Somebody **needs to** / **can't** rescue it, so it doesn't get hurt.

6   I think I **had to** / **will have to** call somebody for help.

Think and Reflect: Unit 8

My understanding of fun ☆☆☆☆☆

How well I achieved my goal for Unit 8 ☆☆☆☆☆

The most interesting thing that I learned ____

My goal for Unit 9 ____

9 How is having fun good for us?

Vocabulary 1

A Complete the sentences.

1 It's fun to see a little green ______________ coming up in the spring.

2 This ______________ is useful for carrying a lot of cups.

3 We made these animals from ______________ in class today.

4 Don't speak too loudly. They might ______________ you.

5 You can write each of your ideas on a ______________ of paper.

6 We do exercises in P.E. class to improve our ______________ .

B Match to make sentences.

1 Tom's very experienced …

2 Tom doubts …

3 Tom has a crucial …

4 Good coordination …

5 Tom's team's training is overseen …

6 It's becoming increasingly …

a he'll ever be a professional player.

b difficult to win games, because the opposing teams are so good.

c job on the team, because he's the goalkeeper.

d because he's been playing ice hockey since he was six.

e by their fantastic coach.

f is important because Tom has to stop very fast shots.

A Check (✓) the correct option.

1 My grandma lives … now, so we often visit her.

☐ alone   ☐ lonely

2 This video game is only $10. That's a very good … .

☐ prize   ☐ price

3 I make sure I'm always on time because I don't like being … .

☐ lately   ☐ late

4 I had so much … last weekend!

☐ funny   ☐ fun

5 I have a friend who always tells really … jokes.

☐ funny   ☐ fun

6 My best friend won a … for her poem about penguins.

☐ price   ☐ prize

7 Who do you call for a conversation when you feel … ?

☐ alone   ☐ lonely

8 I haven't seen any good movies … .

☐ lately   ☐ late

B Underline the past perfect verbs and circle the simple past verbs.

1 We hadn't been out long before the sun began to shine.

2 We went for a bike ride as soon as we'd eaten lunch.

3 Had the store closed when you arrived?

4 They had learned a lot of new words by the time class ended.

5 Had the TV show started before you turned the TV on?

6 Before I found my backpack, I'd looked everywhere!

C Which action happened first? Check (✓).

1 After I had got on the bus, I realized it was the wrong one.

☐ I got on the bus.   ☐ I realized it was the wrong bus.

2 Before I did my homework, I had played soccer and tennis.

☐ I did my homework.   ☐ I played soccer and tennis.

3 By the time I got home, the sun had set.

☐ I got home.   ☐ The sun set.

4 I had said goodnight to my family before I went to bed.

☐ I said goodnight.   ☐ I went to bed.

D **Match the questions to the answers.**

1 Had you been to Australia before? •

2 Had your family ever seen
kangaroos before? •

3 Had your sister taken the picture by
the time the kangaroo disappeared? •

• **a** Yes, it had left right after.
• **b** No, I hadn't. It was my first visit.
• **c** Yes, they had, but only on TV.

E **Complete the sentences with the past perfect form of the verbs in parentheses.**

1 None of my friends _______________ (hear) of an animal
called a quagga before we learned about them at school.

2 The volcano _______________ (form) many thousands of
years earlier.

3 I _______________ (not find) a fossil until I went to that beach.

4 _______________ you _______________ (learn) to swim by the
time you were five?

5 They _______________ (meet) each other when they were at summer camp.

6 After many years, the old house _______________ (fall) down.

F **Write a question for each answer with the past perfect.**

1 <u>Had you ever seen a double rainbow before?</u> _______________
No, I'd never seen a double rainbow before.

2 ____
Yes, we had learned about rainbows in class.

3 ____
No, they hadn't heard the warning about the storm.

4 ____
Yes, they had already packed an emergency bag.

5 ____
No, she had never experienced a hurricane before.

6 ____
Yes, she had watched videos about hurricanes before.

A **Read the story. How did Samantha find her "thing"?**

Samantha Finds Her Thing

"Let's meet up on Sunday," Samantha said to Mayumi.

"Sorry, I can't," replied Mayumi. "I have band practice."

"I'd like a hobby like yours."

"You could learn an instrument, too!" laughed Mayumi. "For me, music's more than a hobby. It's part of who I am."

"I'm not sure music is my thing. But there has to be something that *is*," replied Samantha thoughtfully.

Samantha had always enjoyed watching sports, so she joined a basketball club. After a few sessions, her fitness and coordination had improved, but she wasn't as good as the other players, and she was never selected to play in games. After nine sessions, she'd convinced herself that her fitness wasn't good enough.

"I doubt basketball is ever going to be my thing," said Samantha, sadly.

"Try something creative," suggested Mayumi.

Samantha had always enjoyed art. The next weekend, she watched some online videos to learn how to make papier mâché. Then she created beautiful animals by sticking strips of paper on balloons and adding cardboard pieces to create the different body parts. But she didn't know what to do with all the animals!

"It's lonely doing a hobby on my own. My thing needs to be something I can do with other people," she told Mayumi.

On her way home, Samantha saw her 94-year-old neighbor, Mr. Friedhof. He had always been kind to her family, helping them in the yard, building a fence, and cutting some branches off their trees. Suddenly, Mr. Friedhof dropped his stick and started to lose his balance.

"Let me help you, Mr. Friedhof!" cried Samantha.

"Thank you, Samantha. I should be more careful, but I'm in a hurry! I'm going to Grandfriends."

"What's Grandfriends?" asked Samantha.

"It's a club where older people get together with younger people. It's so much fun!"

Samantha told Mr. Friedhof about her mission to find her thing. "What's your thing?" she asked him.

"I've done many things," he replied. "I've climbed mountains, run businesses, written poems … but the thing I like most is helping other people – that's my thing!"

B **Underline these words in the text.**

strips   coordination   experienced   papier mâché   fitness   doubt

C **Read and circle *True* or *False*.**

1 Samantha decided to learn a musical instrument like her friend Mayumi.   **True**   **False**

2 Samantha quit the basketball club because she thought she wasn't in good enough shape.   **True**   **False**

3 Samantha chose to try papier mâché because she had enjoyed art in school.   **True**   **False**

4 Samantha enjoyed doing a hobby alone.   **True**   **False**

5 Samantha had met Mr. Friedhof before she saw him in the street.   **True**   **False**

6 Samantha found her thing after going to Grandfriends.   **True**   **False**

D **Evaluate the story by answering the questions.**

1 In my opinion, the story was ___________________________________.

2 I wanted to read it to the end because ___________________________________.

3 Samantha's character seemed believable because ___________________________________.

4 I cared what happened to Samantha because ___________________________________.

5 The story taught me that ___________________________________.

Samantha's thing is helping others. What's your thing?

Vocabulary 2

A Circle the correct option.

1 Some people have **anxiety** / **breath** before they take a test at school.

2 There can be a strong **painkiller** / **bond** between friends.

3 You might take a deep **breath** / **workout** before jumping into a swimming pool.

4 You could **cheer up** / **concentrate** a friend who is upset about something.

5 You definitely need to **workout** / **concentrate** when you're riding a bike on a busy road.

6 You might take a **painkiller** / **supportive** if you get a headache.

B Read and complete the paragraph.

> bond   workout   anxiety   concentrate   supportive   breath

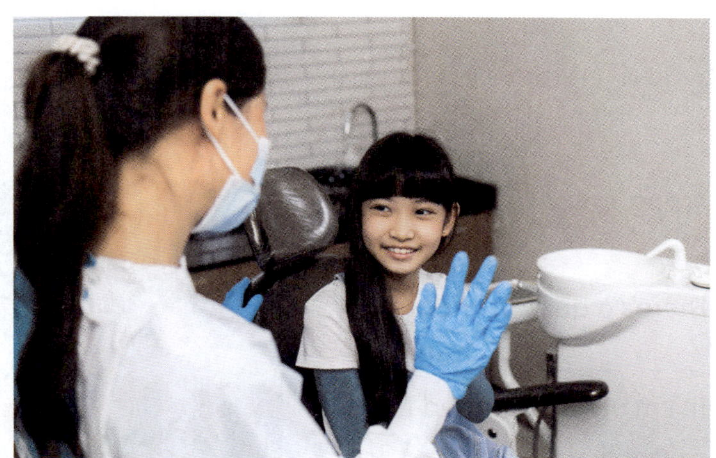

I used to dislike going to the dentist, but I found ways of reducing my [1] ______________ .
First, I reminded myself to take a big [2] ______________ before I walked into the dentist's office.
That helped me to feel calm. Next, I remembered to [3] ______________ really hard on all the things
that make me feel relaxed and happy. For example, I visualized myself playing soccer, which I love.
Then, I thought about doing a laughter [4] ______________ with my friends. I also talked to my
best friend about my feelings because he is always very [5] ______________ and there is a strong
[6] ______________ between us.

C Match to make sentences.

1 It's important to … when you take a test. • • **a** anxiety

2 I have … when I'm in a large crowd. • • **b** supportive

3 He took a … because he had an earache. • • **c** workout

4 There's a strong … between a mother and child. • • **d** concentrate

5 It's important to have caring and … friends. • • **e** painkiller

6 She does a morning … before she goes to school. • • **f** bond

A **Check (✓) the correct option.**

1 I always try to … problems and challenges.

☐ deal with   ☐ retrieve

2 It was fun to … stories in class.

☐ deal with   ☐ make up

3 The students were … by the bird outside the window.

☐ distracted   ☐ motivated

4 We were … to help at last week's fundraiser.

☐ motivated   ☐ memorized

5 Your brain can … old memories easily.

☐ distract   ☐ retrieve

6 I want to … two phone numbers and a poem.

☐ deal with   ☐ memorize

B **Read and complete the dialogue.**

memorize   motivated   retrieve   deal with   distracted

Ali: What's wrong, Milo? You look 1 ________________ .

Milo: I'm OK. There's a quiz on Friday and I don't 2 ________________ quizzes very well! I'm always worried I'll make a mistake.

Ali: It's a vocabulary test, isn't it?

Milo: Yes. I have to 3 ________________ 10 new words in Spanish.

Ali: Do you like learning Spanish?

Milo: Sure, I do! I'm very 4 ________________ to learn it because my cousins live in Girona and I want to go visit them one day.

Ali: I know what we can do! Let's draw a funny picture for each new word you have to learn. My teacher said that using a picture can help your brain 5 ________________ important things more easily.

Milo: OK, that sounds fun! Thanks, Ali.

A Read the poem. Label the different features.

Rhyme   Onomatopoeia   Stanza   Alliteration

Have You Had Some Fun Today?

____

Under our bright and happy sun,

There's a big world of joy and fun.

We'll hike up hills and roll back down,

Chase cheerful clouds all over town.

____

See shooting stars go whooshing by,

As we reach up to touch the sky.

____

We'll splash in puddles when raindrops fall,

Nature's playground welcomes all.

Imagine stories, dream along –

Tell a joke and sing a song.

Smile and laugh, run and be free!

Fun never ends, as you will see.

____

As time flies by, remember this,

Life's full of joys you shouldn't miss.

So have you had some fun today?

"Well, yes, I have," I hear you say.

B Answer the questions.

1 How does the poet organize the poem?

____

2 What are three examples of rhyme in the poem?

____

3 What are two examples of onomatopoeia in the poem?

____

4 What is an example of alliteration in the poem?

____

C You're going to write a poem. Choose a subject and brainstorm ideas.
Use the graphic organizer to help you.

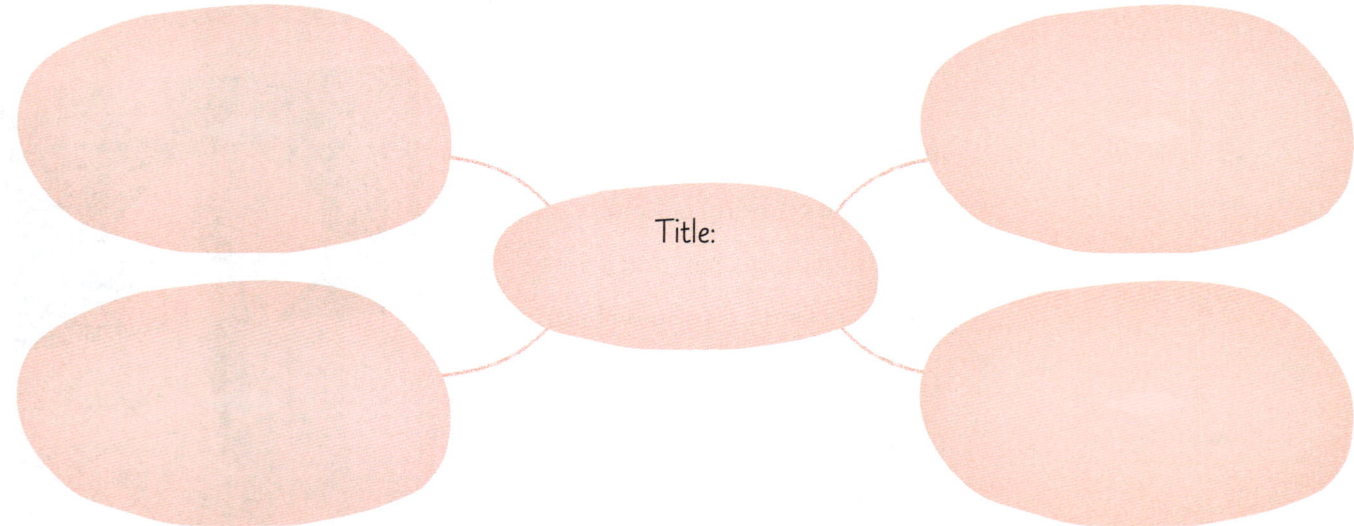

D Outline your best idea by completing the graphic organizer.

E Now write the first draft of your poem in your notebook. 

- Use a title that describes the subject of your poem.
- Organize your poem into stanzas or one piece.
- Include some alliteration and/or onomatopoeia.
- Use full sentences or a mix of full and incomplete sentences.

F Check your work and make any necessary changes.

- Did you do everything in the list in **E**?
- Is your grammar, spelling, and punctuation correct?
- Is your writing clear and easy for other people to understand?

G Now write the final draft of your poem in your notebook. 

A **Unscramble the words to complete the paragraph.**

I really need to ¹ c_____________ (tetraceconn) because I'm doing a difficult math problem, but my best friend is ² d_____________ (tstracgnidi) me. But I don't mind. We have a strong ³ b_____________ (nobd) and we're always ⁴ s_____________ (ropisuptve) toward each other.

B **Circle the correct option.**

1 I **doubt** / **retrieve** that I can run one kilometer in less than two minutes.

2 Yesterday, my head hurt. Mom gave me a **tray** / **painkiller** to help me feel better.

3 We planted some seeds. After a month, I saw one small **shoot** / **coordination** appear.

4 My dad and I go to the gym every Saturday morning because we enjoy improving our **anxiety** / **fitness** .

C **Find the mistakes. Rewrite the sentences using the past perfect.**

1 Were you ever been to Chile before?

____

2 We never flown in a small plane until we went to the islands.

____

3 Why didn't the bus arrived? Was there a traffic jam?

____

4 All my friends had see the movie already, but I hadn't.

____

5 Has the store opened by the time you got there?

____

6 We went for a walk as soon as we had finish our homework.

____

Think and Reflect: Unit 9

My understanding of fun ☆☆☆☆☆

How well I achieved my goal for Unit 9 ☆☆☆☆☆

The most interesting thing that I learned _____________________________________

My goal for Unit 10 _____________________________________

10 How can we assess if something really exists?

A Circle the correct option.

1 The **pins** / **proof** keep the pieces of fabric together while I'm sewing.

2 I've been reading an **account** / **admit** of the first voyage to the moon.

3 They walked across the **suspicious** / **stream** .

4 I was a **coincidence** / **fairy** in the school play.

5 He was really happy with his new **claim** / **hairstyle** .

6 The issue caused a lot of **controversy** / **pin** .

B Read and complete the dialogue.

suspicious   coincidence   admit   account   claim   get away with   proof

A: You ¹ ________________ that Mayada took my T-shirt, but I don't believe you. Do you have any ² ________________ ?

B: Well, no. But she's wearing a new T-shirt identical to the one that you've lost. And I saw her next to your bag at the end of P.E. yesterday.

A: That sounds a little ³ ________________ . But maybe it's just a ⁴ ________________ that her T-shirt is the same as mine. And even if she took it, she probably wouldn't ⁵ ________________ to it. Instead, she'd give a different ⁶ ________________ of what happened. We can't accuse her of taking it if we don't have any evidence.

B: But we shouldn't let her ⁷ ________________ this!

Word Study and Grammar

A **Read and complete the sentences.**

> magical   biological   ethical   skeptical   musical   alphabetical   critical   tropical

1 The girl in the story had ________________ powers. For example, she could instantly speak any language, and she could play incredible tunes on a ________________ instrument that she'd never touched before.

2 There are millions of species in Earth's varied ecosystems, but we find the biggest ________________ diversity in ________________ rainforests.

3 I think we have an ________________ responsibility to keep our planet healthy for the people of the future, but sometimes I'm ________________ that we will be able to do this. We aren't doing a very good job of it at the moment!

4 We developed our ________________ thinking by considering how different people might want the information organized: in date order, in an ________________ list, or in order of importance.

B **Read the paragraph. Underline the passive form of the verbs.**

Many stories have been told of a mysterious creature called the *mokele-mbembe*. If you believe the stories, the mokele-mbembe is sometimes seen in the rainforests of Central Africa. It is described as the size of an elephant, with smooth skin, a long neck and a horn. Some people have wondered if the creature was a dinosaur that had survived when other dinosaurs went extinct. Scientists were sent into the rainforest to look for the creature, but no evidence of its existence has ever been found.

C **We often use the passive when it's obvious who does the action. Who did the action in these sentences?**

1 The meals are cooked from scratch in the restaurant kitchen.   ________________

2 Only one goal was scored.   ________________

3 The medicine has been given to the ill child.   ________________

4 My homework answers have been corrected.   ________________

 Complete the chart. Use the correct tense.

	Active	Passive
1	People sometimes ______________ lies.	Lies are sometimes told.
2	People believe her account.	Her account ______________ .
3	Someone ______________ evidence.	Evidence was collected.
4	Peter saw the clues.	The clues ______________ by Peter.
5	Someone ______________ this book.	This book has been chosen.
6	We have done a lot of work.	A lot of work ______________ .

 Write passive sentences with the present perfect and the words in parentheses.

1 (room / clean up) <u>The room has been cleaned up.</u> _______________

2 (clothes / wash) ____

3 (floor / sweep) ____

4 (project / not / finish) ____

5 (presents / not / give) ____

6 (door / shut) ____

7 (money / spend) ____

8 (chocolates / not / eat) ____

 Rewrite the active sentences as passive sentences. Use the correct tense.

1 People write many books about fairies.

   <u>Many books are written about fairies.</u>

2 Someone has taken photos of a fairy!

   ____

3 People have studied that photo carefully.

   ____

4 People didn't interview the photographer.

   ____

5 Someone kept secret the real story of the photos.

   ____

6 All this time, people haven't known the truth.

   ____

A Read the article. Was the Turk an intelligent machine? Give a reason for your answer.

The Amazing Machine

It was 1826, the year of the world's first photograph. But the people of New York were fascinated by another invention that year. It was a mysterious machine that had recently arrived in the city: a machine that seemed to be able to think, and could play a game of chess!

This unusual machine was called the Turk. It consisted of a cabinet with a chessboard on top, and a wooden, life-sized model of a man. The model's arm could move the chess pieces. And the moves that it made could beat everyone except the world's very best chess players.

The Turk had begun its existence on the other side of the Atlantic almost 60 years earlier. Its inventor, Wolfgang von Kempelen, worked for Empress* Maria Theresa of Austria-Hungary, and he designed the machine to impress her. It certainly achieved its goal! Soon, von Kempelen was demonstrating the Turk's extraordinary powers in other European cities.

Before every game, the audience were shown the cabinet's complicated interior, full of levers and wheels. Everyone agreed that no adult could fit in the space that was left. Some people were convinced that the machine could really plan its own chess moves. But others were more suspicious. They wondered if there could be a tiny chess-playing child inside the cabinet, or if someone outside the cabinet was controlling it. Von Kempelen allowed skeptical people to test the Turk in multiple ways. But no one could find proof that it was not what he claimed: an intelligent machine.

After von Kempelen died, the machine was taken around the U.S.A., Canada, and Cuba, and it attracted many more fans. Sadly, though, it was destroyed in a fire in 1854.

Since then, the Turk's secrets have been revealed. The son of its last owner admitted that there had always been an adult chess player inside! In his account, he described how the person outside opened only one door of the cabinet at a time. As each door was opened, the person inside moved silently around the interior of the cabinet on a special seat to avoid detection.

The Turk was an extremely complicated piece of engineering, and although it wasn't able to think by itself, it inspired the idea of a 'thinking machine' for the first time. This has led to the truly intelligent inventions we see today, so it really was an amazing machine!

Glossary:
Empress = the queen of several countries

B **Underline these words in the text.**

admitted   proof   claimed   account   suspicious

C **Number the events in the order that they happened.**

a ☐ The Turk was taken to New York.

b ☐ Wolfgang von Kempelen invented something to impress Empress Maria Theresa.

c ☐ Wolfgang von Kempelen died.

d ☐ The Turk was destroyed.

e ☐ A truly intelligent machine was invented.

f ☐ Wolfgang von Kempelen deceived a lot of people in Europe.

D **Circle the correct option.**

1 New Yorkers were fascinated by **the world's first photo** / **the Turk**.

2 The wooden man was **smaller than** / **the same size as** a real person.

3 **No one** / **A few people** could win a chess game against the Turk.

4 Empress Maria Theresa **was** / **wasn't** impressed by the Turk.

5 The person inside the cabinet was **an adult** / **a small child**.

6 A special **seat** / **board** helped to keep the person inside the cabinet hidden.

Was it unethical for von Kempelen to trick people as he did? Why? / Why not?

A **Read and circle *True* or *False*.**

1 Squid are sea creatures. True False
2 A legend is an accurate account of a real event. True False
3 A scar may form when a cut in the skin heals. True False
4 Everyone should be as aggressive as possible. True False
5 You can rely on someone who is trustworthy. True False
6 You can drag things along the ground if you tie a rope to them. True False

B **Complete the sentences.**

crew   aggressive   scar   drag   eyewitness   trustworthy

1 To get fit for my expedition in the Arctic, I have to run up hills and ________________ a heavy tire behind me.

2 An ________________ saw the crash and gave evidence to the police.

3 I noticed a man who had blond hair and a ________________ under his eye.

4 The woman was shouting angrily at me, and her body language was very ________________ .

5 You're very ________________ , so I'm happy to lend you my car.

6 A ________________ of three people sailed the yacht across the Atlantic Ocean.

A Complete the sentences.

scientific   hang on   slime   magnetic   headline   watermelon

1 The letters stay on the refrigerator door because they're ______________ .

2 I'd love to do ______________ research when I'm older.

3 You can figure out what the article's about if you read the ______________ .

4 ______________ , you've dropped your doll!

5 We love eating juicy ______________ .

6 The snail left a trail of ______________ behind it.

B Match to make sentences.

1 Something magnetic …   **a** is a gluey liquid.

2 A watermelon …   **b** attracts metal objects.

3 Slime …   **c** is green on the outside and red on the inside.

4 A headline …   **d** if you want them to wait.

5 A scientific theory …   **e** summarizes a news report.

6 Ask someone to hang on …   **f** is an idea that explains the natural world.

A **Complete with the correct punctuation.**

1 "Do you think fairies exist______" asked Shahram.

2 The newsreader said______ "Here are today's headlines______"

3 "Look over there______" she shouted.

4 I whispered______ "Can you see that thing in the water______"

5 Mrs. Hidalgo said______ "You have to think critically______"

B **Complete the sentences. Use the words from the speech bubble, quotation marks, and the correct punctuation.**

1 Ameneh said ______________________ .

2 ______________________ asked Ali.

3 ______________________ the scientist admitted.

C **Write a paragraph from a story about a search for a mysterious animal. Include dialogue with quotation marks.**

Tomas guided the robot camera down into deeper, darker water.

"There's no life in this part of the ocean," he said.

"It's too soon to say that!" said Professor Adebayo.

Suddenly, Tomas spotted something white on the screen.

"Hang on!" he cried. "What's that? Is it a squid tentacle?"

"I've no idea," answered the professor. "But there's definitely a living creature down there."

____

____

____

____

A Unscramble the words to complete the paragraph.

Gloria [1] d_____________ (drgaedg) a cup across the surface of Lake Erie. Then she gave it to another member of the boat's [2] c_____________ (recw), who examined the stinky green [3] s_____________ (ismel) inside. Scientists knew that this disgusting green stuff was made of algae, and that it was killing creatures in the lake. Many people [4] c_____________ (cmielad) that it was caused by fertilizers from farms, which were carried down [5] s_____________ (mtsares) and rivers to the lake. Gloria's [6] s_____________ (sefintciic) expedition was looking for [7] p_____________ (ooprf). It was important that people didn't [8] g_____________ _____________ _____________ (egt ywaa tihw) damaging the lake's precious ecosystem!

B Read and circle the correct option.

1 I love your new **headline** / **hairstyle** / **scar**. Shorter hair looks great on you, and the **pins** / **suspicious** / **claims** that are holding it up are really pretty.

2 There was an **eyewitness** / **admit** / **aggressive** who was able to give a detailed **coincidence** / **fairy** / **account** of the accident.

C Correct the mistakes in the underlined parts of these passive sentences. One sentence doesn't have a mistake.

1 Trustworthy evidence of the monster's existence <u>never been discovered</u>.	_____________

2 The eyewitness <u>was question</u> by the police.	_____________

3 Our account of the discovery <u>has being published</u>!	_____________

4 New evidence <u>is always investigated</u>.	_____________

5 Giant squid <u>have been not seen</u> very often.	_____________

Think and Reflect: Unit 10

My understanding of existence ☆☆☆☆☆

How well I achieved my goal for Unit 10 ☆☆☆☆☆

The most interesting thing that I learned _________________________________

My goal for Unit 11 _________________________________

Vocabulary 1

A Complete the sentences.

> wonder   edge   lump   nonstop   faint   the naked eye

1 You don't need a telescope to look at the moon. You can see it with _______________ .

2 Don't go near the _______________ of the cliff. It's dangerous.

3 The machine in this factory works _______________ . It's on 24 hours a day.

4 I looked carefully at the _______________ of rock to see where it came from.

5 I heard the _______________ sound of a bird singing in the tree.

6 These pyramids are a _______________ of the ancient world.

B Match to make sentences.

1 Let's measure the diameter …   **a** as it took off.

2 Everyone watched the spacecraft …   **b** pieces of plastic in our oceans.

3 We were excited to learn about the origin …   **c** some water on to the grass.

4 Scientists think there may be a trillion …   **d** of this circle.

5 The geyser …   **e** produces a huge column of water.

6 We're going to spray …   **f** of the plants we found on the hike.

A **Complete the sentences with the prefixes *astro-* or *uni-*.**

1 I think I would really like to be an __________naut.

2 __________nomers are people who study objects in space, like the sun, moon, and stars.

3 Studying the __________verse has to be a fascinating job!

4 When I was young, I wanted to learn to ride a __________cycle.

5 We don't have to wear a __________form in my school. We can wear our usual clothes.

6 Patrizio is going to college to study __________nomy.

7 We studied the features of the beautiful, __________que vase.

8 The sun and moon are two well-known __________nomical objects.

B **Read and write *Active* or *Passive*.**

1 Has the spacecraft taken off? ______________

2 Has the equipment been put on board the spacecraft? ______________

3 Have the astronauts checked the engines? ______________

4 Has a spacecraft been sent to explore Saturn? ______________

5 Has Saturn been explored before now? ______________

6 Have you seen pictures of Saturn's rings? ______________

C **Complete the questions with the present perfect passive form of the verbs in parentheses.**

1 ______________ the musicians ______________ what time the concert starts? (tell)

2 ______________ all the tickets for the concert ______________? (sell)

3 ______________ the sound equipment ______________? (check)

4 Why ______________ the lights in the concert hall ______________? (not / turn on)

5 ______________ the stage ______________? (clean)

6 Why ______________ the concert programs ______________ to the audience? (not / give)

D **Read the answers. Then use the present perfect passive to complete the questions.**

1 What type of music ________________________ by the musicians?

   The musicians have played classical music.

2 Who ________________________ as the pianist for their concerts?

   They have selected Jody King as their pianist.

3 Who ________________________ to sing the solos?

   They have invited Luciano Galluzzo to sing the solos.

4 Which days ________________________ for the concerts?

   They have chosen three days in June.

5 Where ________________________ the tickets ________________________?

   They have sold the tickets online.

E **Rewrite the active questions as present perfect passive questions.**

1 Has someone planned our trip?

   ____

2 Has someone left a note for the neighbors?

   ____

3 Hasn't anyone booked our train tickets?

   ____

4 Has anyone packed the suitcases?

   ____

5 Hasn't anyone ordered our breakfast?

   ____

F **Write questions with the present perfect passive.**

1 concert hall / clean   ____

2 music / practice   ____

3 stage / decorate   ____

4 programs / print   ____

5 last tickets / sell   ____

A Read the space magazine article. What differences between Earth and Mars does the article mention?

Marvellous Mars!

Mars can be described as Earth's sibling because although Mars is half the size of Earth, they share some similarities. Mars' days are about as long as our days – just 37 minutes longer. Like Earth, Mars rotates on an axis, and like Earth, it experiences seasons. However, it has some amazing features that are very different from anything on Earth.

1 The Grand Canyon of Mars

Valles Marineris is a system of canyons on Mars. It's the largest canyon system in the solar system, extending over 4,000 kilometers in length. To put that number into perspective, the Grand Canyon (one of the wonders of the world), in the U.S.A. is just 450 kilometers long.

Although we can't see Valles Marineris with the naked eye, it's visible from Earth-based telescopes as well as spacecraft in orbit. It will continue to give us valuable information about the geological processes that shaped the Red Planet over billions of years.

Valles Marineris was named in honor of NASA's Mariner spacecraft missions, especially Mariner 9, which became the first spacecraft to orbit Mars. It made maps of the planet's surface and studied its atmosphere.

Olympus Mons: a massive mountain! 2

Olympus Mons or Mount Olympus is the largest volcano in our solar system and is also located on Mars! It's enormous, with a diameter of about 600 kilometers. That's almost as wide as the whole of France! It's nearly three times as tall as Mount Everest, the highest mountain on Earth. Earth has similar volcanoes, such as Mauna Loa in Hawaii, but none are as big as Olympus Mons!

Did you know that Mars has geysers, too? They're different from geysers on Earth because they spray CO_2 (carbon dioxide), not water.

3 Not just one, but two moons for Mars!

Mars has two moons, Phobos and Deimos. They're both smaller than Earth's moon. Phobos is the larger of the two moons, with a diameter of about 22 kilometers. It's slowly getting closer to Mars. Fifty million years from now, it will either crash into Mars or break apart! Deimos is a little less than half the size of Phobos, with a diameter of about 12 kilometers. You could walk that distance in under three hours.

Mars's moons are potato-shaped and have a lot of craters. Some scientists think they were once asteroids. The gravity on Mars might have captured them into its orbit, turning them into moons. But no one is sure yet!

B **Underline these words in the text.**

> diameter   the naked eye   spray   wonders   geysers   spacecraft

C **Circle the correct option.**

1 Valles Marineris is **bigger than** / **the same size as** the Grand Canyon in the U.S.A.

2 We **can** / **can't** see Valles Marineris with the naked eye.

3 Olympus Mons is a **geyser** / **volcano** on Mars.

4 The geysers on Mars are **the same as** / **different from** those on Earth.

5 Phobos is slowly moving **away from** / **toward** Mars.

D **Read section 1 *The Grand Canyon of Mars* intensively. Answer the questions.**

1 What are the key words in this section? _______________________________

2 Find at least one example of:

   a a present fact   **b** a past event   **c** information about the future

   _______________________   _______________________   _______________________

3 What ideas are described in the main paragraph and the box?

   ____

4 What text features do you notice and what do they help you to understand?

   ____

What new things have been discovered in space since you were born?

A Match to make sentences.

1 Doctors are able to see the inside of your brain … •
2 Your heart is a … •
3 When I broke my arm, the doctor took … •
4 Your brain is inside … •
5 Pain is a … •
6 To protect your head and face from the sun, you can … •

• **a** some X-rays.
• **b** your skull.
• **c** wear a cap.
• **d** by using a scanner.
• **e** very important organ.
• **f** signal that something is wrong with your body.

B Read and circle *True* or *False*.

1 You wear a cap on your head.	**True**	**False**
2 Your heart is inside your skull.	**True**	**False**
3 The brain is an organ.	**True**	**False**
4 X-rays fix broken bones.	**True**	**False**
5 Doctors can do a procedure to make you better.	**True**	**False**
6 Scanners don't show images of inside your body.	**True**	**False**

C Read and complete the paragraph.

scanner   procedure   showed up   signal   X-ray

Last year, my aunt had a stomachache, so she went to see her doctor. She thought it was a
[1] _______________ that she might have health problems. Her doctor gave her an [2] _______________ ,
but it didn't show up anything unusual. So, next her doctor decided to use an endocsope
[3] _______________ to look inside her stomach, and that's when the lump [4] _______________ . My aunt
had to check in to the hospital immediately, so that the doctors could do a [5] _______________ to
remove the lump. Now she feels great!

A Circle the correct option.

1 We used a **building block** / **magnifying glass** to look at the flower's tiny petals.

2 Scientists often work together in a **laboratory** / **microscope**.

3 You can see a lot of detail when you look through a **microscope** / **grain**.

4 It would be impossible to count every **building block** / **grain** of sand on the beach!

5 My little sister is three years old. She loves playing with her colorful **widths** / **building blocks**.

6 Let's measure the **laboratory** / **width** of the door before we try to move the bed out of your bedroom.

B Read and complete the dialogue.

> magnifying glass   laboratory   grain   width   microscope

Jack: Here's a tricky question for you, Paolo. What is the [1] ______________ of a [2] ______________ of salt? Do you have any idea? I'm doing a science quiz.

Paolo: Hmm. I guess it's about half a millimeter, or less! Why don't we measure one?

Jack: OK, but we need a [3] ______________ so we can see it more easily.

Paolo: I'm not sure that will help us. We might need to look at it under a [4] ______________.

Jack: Good idea. There might be one in the science [5] ______________ that we can borrow. I'll go and look.

A Read and circle the correct connector to show result.

My parents have always enjoyed all kinds of sport. [1] **However** / **Consequently** , my brother and I enjoy sport, too. My brother likes sport even more than I do! [2] **That's why** / **Unlike** he's never home. He's always out playing soccer, baseball, tennis, or cricket. He wants to be a professional soccer player one day, [3] **however** / **so** he practices every day. Last month, he played more than 90 hours of sports. [4] **As a result** / **But** he's very tired now.

B Complete the sentences with connectors to show result.

1 I've always loved swimming. _______________ I decided to try snorkeling.

2 Animals are very important to me, _______________ I volunteer at the local animal shelter.

3 I left my lunch at home. _______________ I was very hungry in the afternoon!

4 My tablet needs charging, _______________ I can't use it at the moment.

5 Mom goes to the gym and eats a lot of vegetables. _______________ she looks so healthy.

6 I have a lot of books in my bedroom. _______________ I don't have much space for clothes.

C Write a paragraph about your reasons for learning something. Use connectors to show result.

When I was five, I discovered that I was good at learning languages. My mom is Spanish and my dad is English, so I was raised speaking those two languages. When I was ten years old, we went on vacation to Italy and I loved it! As a result, I asked my parents to download an app and I began learning Italian online. In the last year, I've worked really hard learning a lot of new vocabulary and grammar. That's why now I can speak Italian really well!

____

____

____

____

____

A **Unscramble the words to complete the paragraph.**

My mom is a scientist. She works in a **1** l_____________ (toolbarray) downtown. Every day, she looks at cells under a **2** m_____________ (pomicoscer). Cells are really tiny, but they're the **3** b_____________ _____________ (liidubng closbk) of every part of our bodies. Did you know that you can't see a cell with the **4** n_____________ _____________ (kande yee) because they're not even the **5** w_____________ (ditwh) of a **6** g_____________ (raign) of sand?

B **Circle the correct option.**

1 Most hospitals use **caps** / **X-rays** to look at broken bones.

2 Your heart and lungs are **lumps** / **organs** in your body.

3 What is the **organ** / **origin** of the universe?

4 Your brain sends **trillions** / **procedures** of electrical signals every day.

5 Astronauts use telescopes to try to guess the **diameter** / **wonder** of stars.

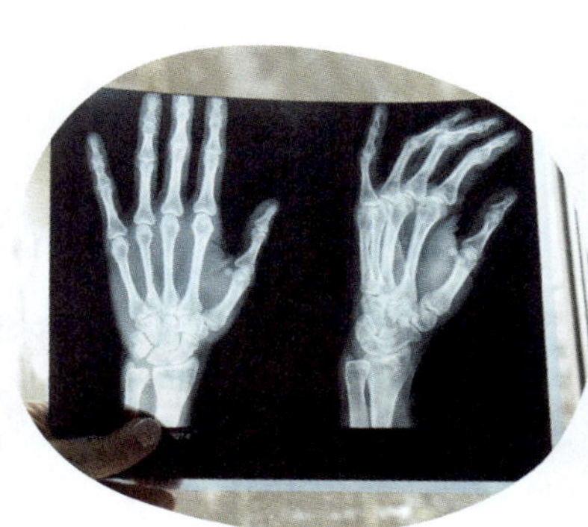

C **Read the answers. Then write present perfect passive questions.**

1 Have the dishes been done?

Yes, someone has done the dishes.

2 ____

No, no one has turned the lights off.

3 ____

Yes, people have prepared lunch.

4 ____

No, no one has put the groceries away.

5 ____

Yes, someone has cleaned up the living room.

Think and Reflect: Unit 11

My understanding of existence ☆☆☆☆☆

How well I achieved my goal for Unit 11 ☆☆☆☆☆

The most interesting thing that I learned ____

My goal for Unit 12 ____

12 How can we find out about existence in the past?

A Complete the sentences.

came across   settlement   remains   arid   sediment   fertile

1 Deserts are ________________ regions with little rain.

2 There's a new ________________ on the edge of the city.

3 Each layer is made of ________________ .

4 This soil is very ________________ .

5 At the market, I ________________ a very interesting picture.

6 They explored the ruined castle's ________________ .

B Match to make sentences.

1 A … is a person who moves from their home to another region.   a vegetation

2 There is a lot of … in wet areas like rainforests.   b depicts

3 We're going to camp in the … next weekend.   c deposited

4 We lit a fire in the … to heat the room.   d migrant

5 If a beach is sandy, the waves have … the sand as sediment.   e wilderness

6 The artist's drawing … the landscape so accurately.   f fireplace

Word Study and Grammar

A **Complete the sentences with the prefix *un-* or *dis-* and these verbs.**

believe   trust   pack   approve   fold   continue

1 She started to ________________ the paper bird. She wanted to figure out how it was made.

2 I got back from my vacation this morning, but I still need to ________________ my suitcase.

3 I ________________ his offer of help. After he's helped me, what will he want in return?

4 My grandparents ________________ of candy. They don't allow it in their house.

5 There's no reason to ________________ her story. She doesn't tend to tell lies.

6 The assistant at the café says I'm the only person that ever buys the lemon cookies. I hope the café doesn't ________________ them!

B **Check (✓) the past perfect sentences that use the passive voice.**

1 ☐ Sediment has been deposited on the ocean floor.

2 ☐ Had art been found in any other caves in the region?

3 ☐ Experts thought the ancient cave art had been painted by talented artists.

4 ☐ When was the cave discovered?

5 ☐ The dead animals had been covered in mud and forgotten for thousands of years.

6 ☐ We hadn't been told about the amazing discoveries.

C **Read and check (✓) the correct answer.**

1 The trees died because the climate had changed.

What changed?   ☐ the climate   ☐ we don't know

2 Mika had been selected for the research project.

Who selected Mika?   ☐ Mika   ☐ we don't know

3 Sediment had been taken to the laboratory.

Who took the sediment?   ☐ the laboratory   ☐ we don't know

4 Safi had lost his laptop.

Who lost the laptop?   ☐ Safi   ☐ we don't know

 Find the mistakes. Rewrite the sentences using the passive voice in the past perfect.

1 They hadn't been give the correct information.

   ____

2 When he had been hurt?

   ____

3 Our school had never be visited by an archeologist before!

   ____

4 I been encouraged to read a book about geology.

   ____

E **Rewrite the active sentences as passive sentences using the past perfect.**

1 Someone had lit a match.

   A match had been lit.

2 No one had brought the balls.

   ____

3 Had anyone done the cleaning?

   ____

4 They hadn't written the report.

   ____

5 Had people seen hippos in that region before?

   ____

6 Someone had grown some flowers.

   ____

F **Complete the active and passive sentences with the past perfect of the verbs in parentheses.**

When I got home from school:

1 My bed _________________________ (make).

2 Dad _________________________ (do) the dishes.

3 The dinner _________________________ (not cook).

4 The dogs _________________________ (not feed).

5 All the orange juice _________________________ (drink).

A Read the encyclopedia pages. What evidence is given for the information about the Americas' first people?

The Americas' First People

25,000 years ago, the continents and islands of the Americas were a wilderness with stunning landscapes and varied vegetation. Their wildlife included mammoths, saber-toothed cats, and giant sloths the size of elephants. But it seems that one species common in most other parts of the world didn't exist in the Americas: humans.

Where did humans come from?

From a biological perspective, we are all Africans. Experts agree that our species – named *Homo sapiens* or 'wise man' – began in Africa around 300,000 years ago. From there, we spread into Asia. By 50,000 years ago, we had reached Australia, and by 40,000 years ago, most of Europe had also been settled.

What about the Americas?

The earliest human settlements that archeologists have come across so far in the Americas are about 15,500 years old. They've been found in North America and as far south as Chile.

Who were these early Americans?

Scientists have studied the genes of a young boy who lived about 12,600 years ago, whose remains were found buried in the north of the U.S.A. Genes are the biological code inside living things, which allows them to pass on their characteristics to the next generation. The boy's genes show that his ancestors had come from Northeast Asia, and that his people were the ancestors of most Native American groups today.

How did people get from Asia to America?

These days, there is ocean between Northeast Asia and Northwest America, but geologists and climate scientists have figured out that 15,500 years ago, sea levels were much lower. At that time, migrants could walk on land that's now underwater.

15,500 years ago, the north of North America was covered in ice. Many experts believe America's first people avoided this ice, and instead spread south along the Pacific coast. If that's true, a lot of the earliest human settlements in the Americas are now on the ocean floor, as they were flooded when sea levels rose.

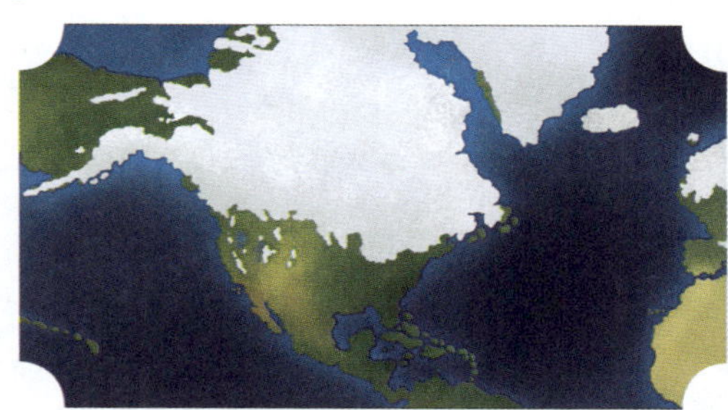

What impact did humans have?

As the human population grew, some large animal species, including mammoths, giant sloths, and saber-toothed cats, disappeared from most parts of the Americas. We don't know why this happened. However, around the world it seems that, soon after humans have reached an area for the first time, many large mammal species have disappeared.

The Americas still have stunning landscapes and varied vegetation. With better care of other species in future, they will continue to be a wonderful place for humans to live.

B **Underline these words in the text.**

> remains   vegetation   wilderness   come across   settlements   migrants

C **Read and circle *True* or *False*.**

1 Our species was in Europe before it was in Africa.   **True   False**

2 Humans lived in Chile more than 15,000 years ago.   **True   False**

3 The ancestors of Native American people came from Northeast Asia.   **True   False**

4 Early Asian people had to build boats to travel to the Americas.   **True   False**

5 There may be the remains of early American human settlements underwater.   **True   False**

6 Humans and giant sloths lived successfully together for many thousands of years.   **True   False**

D **Complete the Venn diagram with information from the encyclopedia pages.**

The Americas before humans arrived

Both

The Americas after humans arrived

What was good and bad about life for the first humans in the Americas?

A **Check (✓) the correct answers. You can sometimes check more than one.**

1 Where can you bathe?

☐ a bathroom   ☐ a river   ☐ a couch

2 What is often made as a loaf?

☐ paint   ☐ cheese   ☐ bread

3 What color are burnt things?

☐ black   ☐ red   ☐ green

4 What do people do in their leisure time?

☐ relax   ☐ do a hobby   ☐ work

5 What do politicians usually do?

☐ help to make laws   ☐ fly planes   ☐ run countries

6 What do people usually go to a stand to do?

☐ send emails   ☐ buy things   ☐ dance

B **Read and complete the paragraphs.**

leisure   loaves   southern   burnt   stand   bathe   politicians   rule

I can't wait to go on vacation. I'm going to the
[1] _______________ coast, where it's really hot. I'm going to
[2] _______________ in the ocean and relax in the sun. I'll have
to remember to put a lot of sunscreen on my skin, because red,
[3] _______________ skin is really painful. It'll be so nice to have
some [4] _______________ time after all my hard work at school
this semester.

Last year, I wanted to raise some money for a wildlife
hospital. I made some [5] _______________ of bread and
started to sell them from a [6] _______________ outside my
house. But I quickly had to stop. I hadn't realized that the
local [7] _______________ who [8] _______________ my city had
made laws against people selling food without permission.
Next time, I'll do more research before I try to sell something!

A **Read and circle *True* or *False*.**

1 A spirit is a creature that exists in the real, visible world. True False

2 A historical record is something that can give us information about the past. True False

3 We usually refuse to do things that we enjoy. True False

4 We might feel jealous of people whose lives seem better than ours. True False

5 If something happens eventually, it happens really quickly. True False

6 We usually want revenge on people who do nice things for us. True False

B **Complete the sentences.**

> eventually   refuse   revenge   spirits   jealous   record

1 I'd love a new bike like yours. I'm so ________________!

2 He'll probably ________________ to help me. He never has time to help.

3 My brother threw a bucket of icy water on me in the yard yesterday, so I'm planning to hide his favorite robot toy for ________________.

4 There's an old man in my neighborhood who says he can communicate with ________________, but no one believes him.

5 Keep a ________________ of how much you spend, so we can pay you back later.

6 It took me a long time to do my history homework, but I finished it ________________.

C **Match to make sentences.**

1 He got in trouble because he …

2 I still haven't solved the puzzle, but I know that I'll solve it …

3 We lost the last time we played this team, so tonight we want …

4 I wish I could solve math calculations as quickly as you! I'm so …

5 She's reading a mystery book about …

6 I exercise a lot, and I keep a …

a jealous.

b spirits.

c refused to help clean up.

d revenge.

e record of my workouts.

f eventually.

A Read the myth. Label the different features.

Resolution   Problem   Title   Reason for something in the world today
Good character(s)   Bad character(s)

The Return of Color

The Father Spirit had finished creating the beautiful Earth and all that lived there, and was admiring his work. He saw blue kingfishers feeding from bubbling streams, red leaves dropping gently from magnificent trees in fall, and the endless green of the zebras' grasslands. He was proud of his creation.

However, the evil spirit Vetanka was jealous of Earth's beauty. "It's not fair that Earth has stunning colors while my spirit land is boring and gray!" she said.

She decided to take what she could while the Father Spirit was visiting his brother far away. First, she took all the red from the world and used it to paint her castle. Then she took the world's orange so that she could have spectacular clothes. She continued with all the other colors. Eventually, her land was so full of bright colors that it hurt the eyes, and Earth was a sad, gray place.

When the Father Spirit returned, he was furious. He filled a giant bucket with water, and threw it over Vetanka's land to wash the color away from it. The color fell back to Earth in raindrops, and Earth became colorful again. Vetanka was washed away, too, and now has to live in the dark water of the deepest ocean.

As the final drops of rain fell to Earth and the color returned, the Father Spirit smiled. He decided to give Earth a present to celebrate the return of its precious colors. He threw a rainbow into the sky!

Even today, the Father Spirit sometimes smiles sunshine onto Earth when he sees rain falling. He remembers the return of color, and the sky is decorated with a beautiful rainbow.

B Answer the questions.

1 What thing in the world today does the myth explain?

____

2 What's the problem in the story?

____

3 How is the problem resolved?

____

 You're going to write a myth that explains something in the world today. Brainstorm. Write your ideas in the graphic organizer below.

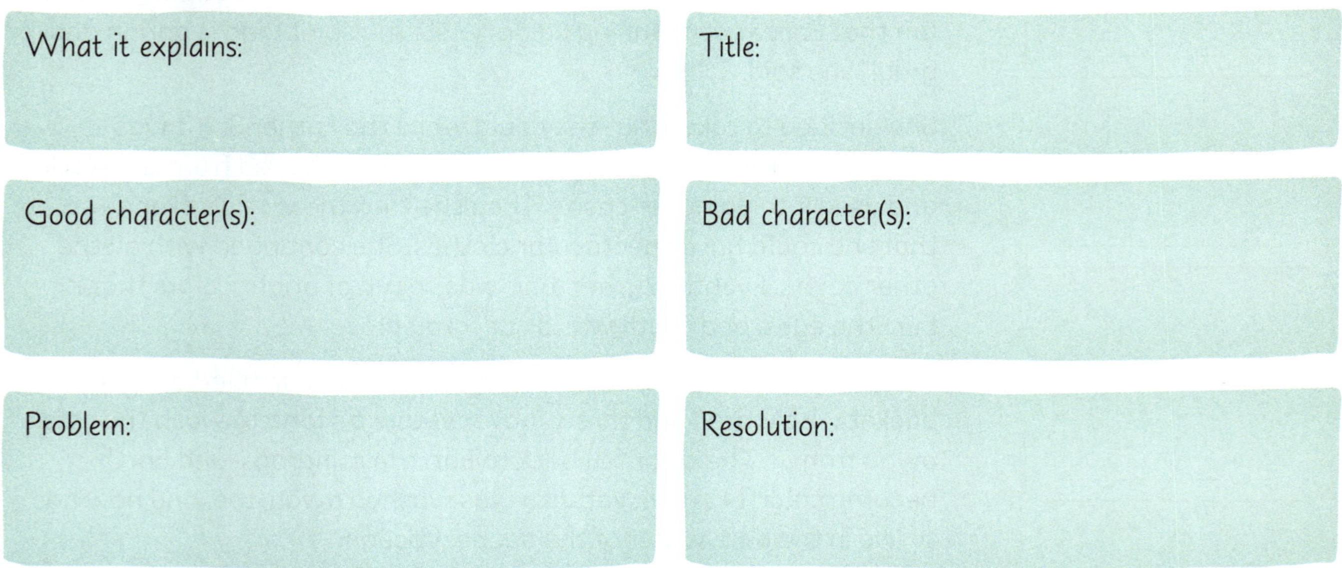

D **Outline your best idea by completing the chart.**

What it explains:	Title:
Good character(s):	Bad character(s):
Problem:	Resolution:

E **Now write the first draft of your myth in your notebook.** 

- Describe the characters.
- Include a problem that the good characters face.
- Say how the problem is resolved.
- Connect the story to something in the real world today.

F **Check your work and make any necessary changes.**

- Did you do everything in the list in **E**?
- Is your grammar, spelling, and punctuation correct?
- Is your writing clear and easy for other people to understand?

G **Now write the final draft of your myth in your notebook.** 

A Read and circle the correct option.

The [1] **southern** / **leisure** / **revenge** city of Sydney is Australia's biggest [2] **stand** / **settlement** / **bathe** and it has a strange history. From 1788, it was [3] **ruled** / **refused** / **come across** by the British. Most of the people who lived there had been sent from Britain as a punishment for their crimes. There are still [4] **remains** / **records** / **politicians** of these people's names. At first, they weren't happy that they had been forced to become [5] **fireplaces** / **migrants** / **sediment**, but [6] **wilderness** / **loaf** / **eventually** many of them decided to stay.

B Unscramble the words to complete the sentences.

1 My favorite picture is above the f______________ (fepclirea) in my living room. It d______________ (dicstep) a vase of colorful flowers.

2 No one will want to eat those l______________ (aveosl) of bread. They're completely b______________ (unrbt).

C Read and complete the paragraphs. Use the active or passive voice and the past perfect form of the verbs in parentheses.

In 1812, Johann Burckhardt walked through a gap in the rocks of the desert.
[1] ______________ he ______________________________ (trick) by his Arab friends, who
[2] ______________________________ (tell) him about an ancient city? He could find nothing except wilderness here. *Perhaps I should turn back*, he thought. But then he saw beautiful buildings glowing red in the sunlight!

He [3] ______________________________ (come) to a very old city called Petra.
It [4] ______________________________ (build) by ancient Arab people called the Nabateans.
Its buildings [5] ______________________________ (carve) into the rocky mountains, in a style that the Nabateans [6] ______________________________ (copy) from Greek architecture. Today, Petra is Jordan's most popular tourist attraction.

My understanding of existence ☆☆☆☆☆

How well I achieved my goal for Unit 12 ☆☆☆☆☆

The most interesting thing that I learned ____

My goal for Unit 13 ____

Vocabulary 1

A   **Read and complete the dialogues.**

> sensible   sibling   privacy   addition   ridiculous   fault   tons of   bassinet

A: Who is that baby in the [1] _______________ ?

B: It's the new [2] _______________ to Nayla's family. I'm not sure if it's a boy or a girl, but I think she's so lucky to have a baby [3] _______________ !

A: Oh no! You just broke Grandma's statue.

B: I know. But it wasn't my [4] _______________ . It was on the edge of the table!

A: There are [5] _______________ people in our apartment!

B: I know. It's very hard to get any [6] _______________ right now.

A: My little brother is wearing [7] _______________ clothes today!

B: Yes, but that's because he's very young. Sometimes he isn't very [8] _______________ .

B   **Circle the correct option.**

1   "I'm so sad," said Billy with a **sibling** / **sigh** .

2   There's no **addition** / **limit** to the love that you can give people.

3   A lot of my mom's time is **occupied** / **ridiculous** with running her business, so she doesn't have much time to relax.

4   Could you just **glance** / **fault** at the clock and tell me what time it is?

5   My older sister is very **sensible** / **sibling** . She studies every day.

A **Complete the sentences.**

> in   about   to   from   of   on

1 Our teacher insists _______________ students being kind and polite.

2 We've run out _______________ milk. Let's put it on the grocery list.

3 Do you know who this bicycle belongs _______________?

4 I plan on competing _______________ the next race.

5 Did you hear that a monkey has escaped _______________ the nature reserve?

6 Dad doesn't like it when I complain _______________ eating vegetables.

B **Check (✓) the sentences that use the future passive.**

1 ◯ The app will be downloaded.

2 ◯ The judges will award a prize.

3 ◯ The grass won't be cut on Saturday.

4 ◯ We'll be woken up by birds singing.

5 ◯ Who will take us to school?

6 ◯ When will the movie be shown?

C **Read the paragraph. Circle the correct option.**

Loaloa and Maya are visiting the pyramids for the first time. They will be picked up after breakfast on Monday. They'll be taken by bus to Giza, just outside the city. They won't be told about the history of the pyramids until they're on the bus. Then, they'll find out about the pharaohs and how the pyramids were built. When they arrive at Giza, they'll be introduced to their guide, Sami. Next, they'll be shown the Sphinx and the Great Pyramid. They'll be asked not to touch the ancient ruins because that can cause a lot of damage.

There are **four** / **six** / **eight** future passive words.

D **Read the passive sentences and complete the active sentences.**

1 Loaloa and Maya will be picked up after breakfast.

Someone _______will pick_______ Loaloa and Maya up after breakfast.

2 They will be taken by bus to Giza.

A bus _____________________ them to Giza.

3 They'll be told about the history of the pyramids.

The driver _____________________ them about the history of the pyramids.

4 They'll be introduced to their guide, Sami.

Someone _____________________ them to their guide, Sami.

5 They'll be shown the Sphinx and the Great Pyramid.

Sami _____________________ them the Sphinx and the Great Pyramid.

E **Look and write sentences with the future passive.**

1 suitcases / pack / ?

____

____

2 guidebook / read

____

____

3 flights / book

____

____

F **Read and complete the paragraph with the future passive form of the verbs in parentheses.**

I've decided to change my life! I'm going to start a lot of good, new habits. My bedroom
1 _____________________ (clean) every morning. My bed 2 _____________________
(make) as soon as I'm dressed and it 3 _____________________ (not leave) messy ever
again! My school books 4 _____________________ (place) neatly on the shelf. My homework
5 _____________________ (do) right after dinner every school day. My school uniform
6 _____________________ (hang) in the closet every evening. The TV in the living room
7 _____________________ (not leave on) so it won't waste energy anymore. And every day,
the breakfast dishes 8 _____________________ (do) … by me!

What will be done in your bedroom
before you go to school tomorrow?

Truffle Trouble!

At 1:00 a.m., Marcel arrived at the edge of the forest. The air smelled of wet leaves and he could hear strange noises in the distance.

I need to start hunting before Luc arrives, thought Marcel. *Today, I'll find every truffle that's here.*

The forest was famous for black truffles – a special type of delicious mushroom that grew underground. Everyone was occupied by the thought of eating truffles, but only Luc and Marcel knew where to find them! If you found fresh truffles at night, you could sell them in the market the next day. There was no limit to the money you might make. However, it was lonely in the forest, and a little frightening.

At 5:00 a.m., Marcel had three small truffles in his basket. Suddenly, he heard a noise nearby that made him jump.

"Hello!" laughed Luc.

"Oh! It's only you!" Marcel said with a big sigh.

"You should quit, Marcel," said Luc. "It's not your fault, but you're a terrible truffle hunter. I have tons of the best truffles anyone ever saw. You'll never beat me."

"But how? You must know something I don't!" replied Marcel. "And that's unfair."

Luc smiled. "I can only tell you this, Marcel. I have a new addition to my family. He's the best!"

Night after night, Marcel found a few truffles, but Luc found many more. The market was full of fresh black truffles, but they were all Luc's.

Late one night, Marcel went out into the forest to discover what Luc's secret was. He climbed a tree and waited patiently. Hours passed, but nothing happened. Suddenly, he heard digging noises under the tree … and then, barking. To his astonishment, he saw a small dog, digging and digging.

"Good job, Bruno!"

Marcel immediately recognized Luc's voice!

"That's the biggest truffle you've found tonight! Good boy!"

Marcel leaped out of the tree.

"Luc! Is your new addition … a dog? A truffle-hunting dog?" he asked.

"Yes, Marcel. This is Bruno, the best truffle hunter in town. Hey, I have an idea for you."

"Oh?" said Marcel nervously. "What?"

"Bruno has a sister named Tonks," replied Luc. "But I can't work with two dogs at the same time. Maybe we can work together, all four of us! We'll be the best black truffle hunters in the country … maybe even the world."

"I can't wait to meet Tonks," said Marcel, smiling from ear to ear.

B **Underline these words in the text.**

tons of   limit   occupied   fault   sigh   addition

C ⚙ **Read the story again. Visualize as you read. Then choose one scene from the story and write a paragraph describing its sights, sounds, and smells.**

____

____

____

D **Read and circle *True* or *False*.**

1   At the beginning of the story, Marcel and Luc are collaborating.   True   False

2   Only two people know where to find the truffles.   True   False

3   Every night, Luc finds more truffles than Marcel.   True   False

4   One night, Marcel follows Luc into the forest.   True   False

5   Marcel knows from the beginning that Luc has a truffle-hunting dog.   True   False

6   Luc and Marcel agree to hunt together with two dogs.   True   False

When have you collaborated with a friend? What did you do?

A **Circle the correct option.**

1 Many of my favorite clothes are made from **cotton** / **colony**.

2 Grandma likes to wear this necklace because it has a beautiful **army** / **jewel**.

3 The country's **rebellion** / **army** is highly trained.

4 Some people have a strong **desire** / **cotton** to eat sweet things.

5 The Romans came from Italy, but they ruled an **empire** / **jewel** that went from Portugal to Iraq.

6 Many people who didn't like the Roman empire started **famines** / **rebellions** and fought to be independent.

B **Read and complete the paragraph.**

colony   rebellion   famine   jewels   army   cotton   desire

A long time ago, the people of Avarus had a strong [1] ______________ to add new resources to their country. They believed that the neighboring country, Geitonikos, had a lot of precious [2] ______________ underground, so they decided to start a [3] ______________ there. They thought the people of Geitonikos would be angry and that there might be a [4] ______________. They took their [5] ______________ with them in case they needed to fight. However, when they arrived in Geitonikos, they got a big surprise. There was almost nothing there! All the crops in the country kept dying. Only [6] ______________ still grew there and no one could eat that! The people of Geitonikos were hungry because of the terrible [7] ______________. The people of Avarus felt sad, so instead they asked their soldiers to help.

A Complete the sentences.

irrigation   flow   dry up   reservoir   limited   resentful

1 All rivers _______________ into the ocean.

2 Sometimes I feel _______________ when I can't play video games with my sister.

3 Water is a _______________ resource in many places.

4 We need _______________ to grow plants in hot countries.

5 This _______________ supplies water to the city of New York.

6 The strong sun this summer made the lake _______________ a lot.

B Read and circle *True* or *False*.

1 A reservoir is a place where we can store water.   True   False

2 Things that dry up look extremely wet.   True   False

3 Blood flows around the human body.   True   False

4 You're really happy when you feel resentful.   True   False

5 Irrigation is useful in places where it doesn't rain much.   True   False

6 If you use all of a limited resource, more will be produced.   True   False

A **Complete the sentences with the correct form of the verbs in parentheses.**

1 No one in my class _______________ (like) drinking soda.

2 Several neighbors _______________ (be) good friends of my family.

3 _______________ (be) all our cousins coming to stay this summer?

4 Where _______________ (be) everyone?

5 Many people _______________ (like) playing sports.

6 Hardly anyone I know _______________ (be) scared of spiders.

B **Check (✓) the option that can replace the underlined word.**

1 Several students are fundraising for the local animal shelter.

☐ Some   ☐ All

2 A lot of my friends enjoy listening to music.

☐ Few   ☐ Many

3 Every person needs food and water.

☐ No one   ☐ Everyone

4 Not many people drop trash these days.

☐ Every   ☐ Few

5 No one likes getting wet in a storm.

☐ Several   ☐ No person

6 Some students are studying for the quiz.

☐ All   ☐ Several

C **Write a paragraph about you and your friends. Talk about what you like and dislike doing. Use phrases to describe numbers of people.**

I have a lot of friends. Many of them go to the same school as me, but some live further away so I don't see them often. Several friends like being outdoors, enjoying nature. Hardly anyone I know wants to stay home all the time. It's a lot more fun going for a hike or playing a sport outside in the fresh air. Last week, we did a survey of leisure activities in class. No one said they liked golf but everyone said they enjoyed swimming and biking!

____

____

____

____

____

A Read and circle the correct option.

I come from a big family. I have five [1] **jewels / empires / siblings** and we usually have [2] **tons of / bassinets / rebellions** fun together. Of course, like all families, we also have occasional [3] **empire / ridiculous / sensible** arguments. I remember one day we were playing with an [4] **army / irrigation / addition** of toy soldiers. I accidentally broke one, but my brothers and sisters said it was my [5] **colony / famine / fault**. We had to stop the game because everyone was shouting.

B Unscramble the words to complete the sentences.

1 During the summer, the stream in this forest often d____________ ____________ (rides pu).

2 In Ireland, in the middle of the 1800s, there was a f____________ (meafin). Many people left the country to survive.

3 Australia was a British c____________ (yoclon) until 1901.

4 Three of my favorite T-shirts are made of c____________ (noottc).

C Rewrite the active sentences as passive sentences.

1 Someone will organize our party.

____

2 Will someone bake a cake?

____

3 People won't put up decorations.

____

4 Will someone send invitations?

____

5 People will play music.

____

Think and Reflect: Unit 13

My understanding of conflict ☆☆☆☆☆

How well I achieved my goal for Unit 13 ☆☆☆☆☆

The most interesting thing that I learned ____

My goal for Unit 14 ____

14 What can happen as a result of conflict?

Vocabulary 1

A Complete the sentences.

weakened   swirled   swept away   roared

1 As they danced, their long skirts _______________ around their legs.

2 The old bridge used to be strong, but time has _______________ it.

3 The lion _______________ to warn other animals to stay away.

4 The seeds were _______________ in the wind.

B Circle the correct option.

1 Concrete is often used to make **buildings** / **food**.

2 Parallel lines **sometimes** / **never** cross.

3 If you defeat the opposing player, you **win** / **lose**.

C Complete the second sentence so its meaning is similar to the first one.

settle on   hardly ever   rewarding   flee   villagers

1 We must decide what to do. → We must _______________ a plan.

2 She lives in the village. → She's one of the _______________.

3 I almost never watch TV. → I _______________ watch TV.

4 The mouse tried to run away. → The mouse tried to _______________.

5 His job makes him happy. → He has a very _______________ job.

A **Underline and replace one word in the sentences with these synonyms.**

thankful   collapse   delight   force   triumph   terrifying

1 We are really proud of our victory.   ____________

2 Everyone could see his happiness when his brother returned safely.   ____________

3 We are worried that the bridge might fall into the river.   ____________

4 We heard a frightening noise in the darkness.   ____________

5 I was so grateful that I was rescued.   ____________

6 The power of the wind can flatten a forest.   ____________

B **Read and write *Active* or *Passive*.**

1 Has the storm ended yet?   ____________

2 New homes were built.   ____________

3 The cliff had been destroyed.   ____________

4 More information will be announced soon. ____________

5 The new village won't be so near the cliff. ____________

6 Had the ocean's power been defeated?   ____________

C **Complete the sentences with the information in parentheses. Use the passive voice with the correct verb form and *by*.**

1 The views _have been photographed by tourists_ .

   (Tourists have photographed them.)

2 The meeting ________________________________.

   (Mr. Faheem has organized it.)

3 The cliff ________________________________.

   (The storm hadn't weakened it.)

4 The missing book ________________________________.

   (Lena has found it.)

5 The candy ________________________________.

   (The children had eaten it.)

6 ________________ the walls ________________________________?

   (Will Yuxi paint them?)

D Look at the plan for organizing a village party. Make passive sentences about each job. Use the present perfect if the job has already been done, and the future if it hasn't been done yet.

Carmen	make the lemonade ✓
Mateo	bake the cookies ✓
Alvaro	decorate the hall
Valentina	invite the villagers ✓
Leo and Sara	play music
Triana and Jorge	clear up the hall

1 The lemonade has been made by Carmen.

2 ___________________________________

3 ___________________________________

4 ___________________________________

5 ___________________________________

6 ___________________________________

E Read and complete the paragraph.

will be taught   are made   have been found
has been formed   had been reshaped   was swept away

Mons Klint is a breathtaking coastline in Denmark. Its white cliffs
[1] ___________________________ of chalk. This chalk [2] ___________________________
from the shells of microscopic sea creatures that lived on the sea floor millions of years ago. If you visit the area's museum, you [3] ___________________________ about the geology of the dramatic cliffs, and about the interesting fossils that [4] ___________________________ there. But if you hike the coastal trails, be careful. A large piece of cliff [5] ___________________________ in 2007, and before that, the coast [6] ___________________________ many times by the powerful forces of nature.

F Rewrite the active sentences as passive sentences.

1 Will the storm put the villagers in danger?

____

2 Someone had discovered a crack in the rock.

____

3 My soccer coach hasn't chosen me for the team.

____

The Flood, the Cat, and the Baby

It was a cold November night, and the wind was howling angrily outside. Maarten shivered. *I'm glad the cows have been put in the barn*, he thought. *They'll be kept safe in there.*

The wind was shaking his window now, threatening to tear it away from its home and into the swirling dark night air. But the window held on bravely to the wall. The wind's violent attack couldn't defeat it.

Suddenly, there was a furious roar outside. Had the river broken through the dike*? Maarten was afraid that greedy flood waters would sweep away the barn, the house, and his family. He had been told about floods like this in the past. But the flood waters didn't come that night. By morning, the wind had calmed down. The storm was over.

Relieved, Maarten and his father took the cows to graze. Large pieces of roof and fence were lying on the fields. It had certainly been a destructive night!

Maarten climbed up the dike, curious to see what had happened in the next village. The view hit him like a punch in the stomach. There was water as far as his eyes could see! He remembered the huge roar from the night before. *That was the noise of the river flooding the village*, he thought. He was afraid for his friends there.

Suddenly, he noticed something floating nearby. He realized that it was a baby's bassinet, and wondered sadly what had happened to the baby. But what was that on top of the bassinet? A cat! The animal was moving nonstop from one side of the bassinet to the other. What was it doing? Maarten watched the flood water circle the bassinet hungrily, and hoped the cat would be OK.

Suddenly, a small cry reached Maarten's ears. That wasn't the sound of a cat. It was a baby!

He and his father used a piece of broken fence to pull the wooden bassinet to shore. The baby inside stopped crying and gave them a big smile.

"Dad, the cat was keeping the bassinet upright so the baby didn't fall out," said Maarten. "The cat saved the baby's life!"

Many villagers had died in the terrible flood, and others had to flee the area. But the incredible story of the cat and the baby spread. It inspired people to rebuild their lives.

Glossary:
dike = a long, thick wall that stops water from flooding the land

B **Underline these words in the text.**   roar   villagers   flee   sweep away   defeat   swirling

C **Circle the correct option.**

1   The storm **pulled** / **didn't pull** Maarten's window off the wall.

2   Maarten was scared that the **river** / **ocean** would sweep away his house.

3   The roar that Maarten heard was the noise of **the cows** / **the flood**.

4   The village that Maarten saw from the dike was **safe** / **flooded**.

5   The baby's bassinet **floated** / **sank** in the water.

6   The **cat** / **baby** had kept the bassinet balanced.

D **How is personification used in this story? Complete the chart.**

	What is personified?	What word or phrase achieves this?
1 The wind was howling angrily outside.		
2 The wind was shaking his window now, threatening to tear it away from its home and into the swirling dark night air.		
3 Maarten was afraid that greedy flood waters would sweep away the barn, the house, and his family.		
4 But the window held on bravely to the wall.		
5 Maarten watched the flood water circle the bassinet hungrily.		

What natural disasters happen in your country?
What can people do to stay as safe as possible?

A **Match the sentences.**

1 She has lost a lot of blood.
2 Watch out!
3 She wants to make her country better.
4 She makes car seats.
5 She uses a wheelchair.
6 Her refrigerator is broken.

a She works for a vehicle manufacturer.
b She needs a transfusion.
c She works in politics.
d She has a disability.
e She has to buy canned food.
f She has a weapon.

B **Check (✓) the correct option.**

1 Next month there'll be … to choose the best politicians for the country.

☐ a transfusion   ☐ an election

2 … food stays good to eat for much longer than fresh food.

☐ Politics   ☐ Canned

3 Someone might use that … to hurt people.

☐ weapon   ☐ election

4 I moved to this city three years ago, and I've lived here … .

☐ ever since   ☐ canned

5 Because of my … , I need someone to carry my school bag for me.

☐ manufacturer   ☐ disability

6 That factory smells delicious because it belongs to a chocolate … .

☐ manufacturer   ☐ ever since

7 Doctors need to know your blood type before they can give you a … .

☐ weapon   ☐ transfusion

8 Air pollution is an important issue in my country's … at the moment.

☐ disability   ☐ politics

What's your favorite canned food? Why?

A **Circle the correct option.**

1 Don't be impolite. You must talk to people **differ** / **respectfully** .

2 I'd like lemonade, please. Oh, wait, can I **turn into** / **change my mind** and have orange juice instead?

3 He has a strange **belief** / **counselor** about spiders. He thinks they are visitors from another planet!

4 When will the caterpillar **turn into** / **change its mind** a butterfly?

5 Talking to a **belief** / **counselor** might help you to feel less anxious.

6 How do moths **differ** / **respectfully** from butterflies? Are they just butterflies that are active at night?

B **Read and complete the dialogue.**

> turn into   respectfully   change your mind   differ   beliefs

A: A lot of your friend Sujith's opinions [1]________________ from yours. Does this cause any problems in your friendship?

B: No, never! That's because we always talk about our opinions [2]________________. In fact, a disagreement can often [3]________________ a fascinating discussion about our [4]______________.

A: Do you ever [5]______________ after a discussion with Sujith?

B: Hardly ever, but it's happened once or twice.

A **Check (✔) the option that best explains the sentence.**

1 I love swimming in the ocean **unless** the water's really cold.

   a ☐ I only like swimming in the ocean if the water's really cold.

   b ☐ I don't like swimming in the ocean if the water's really cold.

2 You can see a movie **as long as** you've cleaned your room first.

   a ☐ You can't see a movie if you haven't cleaned your room first.

   b ☐ It doesn't matter if you clean your room first or not. You can definitely see a movie.

3 The project will be difficult **even if** we have help.

   a ☐ The project won't be difficult if we have help.

   b ☐ It doesn't matter if we have help or not. The project will definitely be difficult.

B **Circle the correct option.**

1 We'll be late **unless** / **as long as** we walk faster.

2 I'll be upset **even if** / **if** I fail the test.

3 They'll succeed **even if** / **as long as** they work hard.

4 **As long as** / **Even if** the boat sinks, we'll be safe because we're wearing life vests.

5 **Unless** / **If** you're invited to join, you can't be in the club.

C **Write a paragraph about an issue that causes disagreements in your home. Use connectors to show condition.**

One issue that causes disagreements in my home is chores.
As long as I do my chores, my parents let me play video games.
But if I don't do them, I'm not allowed. My mom thinks it's
a good idea to do chores immediately after school. She thinks
that, unless I do them then, I'll forget about them. I disagree.
I'm often too tired immediately after school. But I'll do them at
some time in the day, even if I don't do them when she wants.

____

____

____

____

____

A **Read and circle the correct option.**

When I was a child, I really wanted to be a doctor. But after college, I [1] **turned into** / **changed my mind** / **swept away**. Instead, I [2] **weakened** / **swirled** / **settled on** a new ambition: to work in [3] **belief** / **villager** / **politics**. I won my first [4] **election** / **counselor** / **concrete** ten years ago, and I've been a politician [5] **respectfully** / **hardly ever** / **ever since**. It has been very [6] **canned** / **rewarding** / **parallel** because I can make a difference to people's lives.

B **Unscramble the words to complete the sentences.**

1 I've h______________ ______________ (r d l a h y v e r e) seen the ocean because it's very far away.

2 The dam that blocks the river is made of c______________ (o c t e n c r e).

3 They're building a road p______________ (l a l p e l r a) to the river.

4 The superhero's powers will w______________ (e a w e n k) if her long hair is cut.

C **Rewrite the active sentences as passive sentences.**

1 We've discussed the issue.

____

2 No one had told me.

____

3 Will people make a decision?

____

4 Have they sent it?

____

5 Toni will find a solution.

____

My understanding of conflict ☆☆☆☆☆

How well I achieved my goal for Unit 14 ☆☆☆☆☆

The most interesting thing that I learned ____

My goal for Unit 15 ____

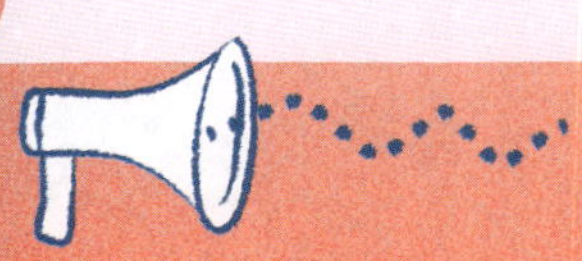

Vocabulary 1

A Read and circle the correct option.

1 The Angolan **representative** / **court** spoke well in the meeting, but later he had to go home urgently because of a family **civilian** / **crisis**.

2 The **prevent** / **court** had several judges who listened to the lawyers' arguments and then decided what to do about the **civilian** / **dispute**.

3 Discussing your problem with a friend might **enable** / **dispute** you to **resolve** / **violence** the situation.

4 **Stick to** / **According to** my doctor, anyone who rides a bike should wear a helmet to **long-term** / **prevent** serious head injuries.

B Complete the second sentence so its meaning is similar to the first one.

> stick to   long-term   violence   civilian   according to

1 We shouldn't change the plan. → We should ______________ the plan.

2 He isn't in the army. → He's a ______________ .

3 The problem has existed for many years. → It's a ______________ problem.

4 My dad says everything will be fine. → ______________ my dad, everything will be fine.

5 This is a very peaceful place. → There isn't any ______________ here.

A **Complete the sentences. Use the adjectives made from these nouns with the suffixes -ful and -less. Use some of these adjectives twice.**

respect   pain   stress   wonder   harm   color

1 I've had a _______________ day, with a lot of difficult situations to deal with.

2 I was worried that getting a filling at the dentist would hurt, but it was completely _______________.

3 The room had been decorated with a lot of _______________ balloons.

4 Your sister had a baby? Congratulations! That's _______________ news!

5 When you visit other countries, you should be _______________ of the local people's traditions.

6 I used to be scared of moths, but now they don't worry me. I know they're _______________.

7 You can't see oxygen because it's _______________.

8 Sunburn can have a _______________ long-term effect on your skin.

B **Read and circle the correct option.**

1 If the sun shines on ice, it melts.

   The sentence is referring to a situation that happens **once** / **many times** .

   What happens because of the situation is **the same** / **different** every time.

2 If Dasha makes a good speech, she'll persuade people.

   The sentence is referring to the **present** / **future** .

   It's **likely** / **unlikely** that Dasha's speech is good.

3 If Salman was Venezuelan, he would speak Spanish.

   The sentence is referring to the **past** / **present** .

   It's **possible** / **impossible** that Salman is Venezuelan.

4 Yasmin would have to wear a blue helmet if she became a UN peacekeeper.

   The sentence is referring to the **past** / **future** .

   It's **likely** / **unlikely** that Yasmin will become a UN peacekeeper.

C **Which conditional do the sentences use? Write.**

zero   first   second

1 If it rains, people get wet. (_______________ conditional)

2 If they came, we'd welcome them. (_______________ conditional)

3 She'll start a campaign if the situation doesn't improve soon. (_______________ conditional)

4 The UN prevents violent conflict if it can. (_______________ conditional)

5 If I wrote to some politicians, would they answer? (_______________ conditional)

6 Will I be able to vote if there's an election soon? (_______________ conditional)

 Match to make sentences.

1 I won't need these sneakers …   **a** if I had a choice.

2 If Matt goes surfing in the winter, …   **b** we won't go to the beach.

3 I wouldn't live in this city …   **c** if they don't get enough water.

4 If it rains, …   **d** I'd buy a new computer.

5 Plants die …   **e** if I don't run in the race.

6 If I had enough money, …   **f** he wears a warm wetsuit.

 Complete the sentences with the correct form of the verbs in parentheses.

1 I ________________________ (complain) if he's late again.

2 ________________________ (you, tell) me if you hated my new hairstyle?

3 If it ________________________ (snow), does the landscape look beautiful?

4 We get hungry if we ________________________ (not eat) by 8:00 p.m.

5 If I ________________________ (forget) to pack something, I'll borrow what I need from a friend.

 Write sentences about these situations. Use the words and the zero, first, or second conditional.

1 if / be / at home / not feel / so cold

____

2 we / not get / to school on time / if / the bus / not come / soon

____

3 I / like / that car / more / if / it / not be / so colorful

____

4 if / you / not stir / the onions / they / burn

____

5 if / I / miss / the train / I / have to / walk / a long way

____

If you could make one change in the world, what would it be? Why?

A Read the Q&A magazine article. Which UN project would be good for a young person who:

a likes creating online content?   **b** wants to practice public speaking?

The United Nations – Get Involved!

A lot of adults help the UN's work, but how can children get involved?

There are several options. Two really good ways are through Model United Nations, and through the Voices of Youth project.

What's Model United Nations?

Model United Nations brings young people together in groups to discuss a world issue in the same way that real UN groups do. For example, they might discuss how to reduce global warming, or how to prevent future pandemics. Each person takes the part of a representative from a different country, and presents ideas from that country's perspective. They try to reach an agreement on what to do.

I'd love to do something like that, but isn't it difficult?

It's important to do some research to prepare for the discussion. If you don't know much about the issue or your country's situation, you won't have much success. But you learn a lot from participating in the Model United Nations. You improve your ability to express arguments clearly, and to challenge other people's arguments respectfully. You also learn from experience that listening is as important as speaking. If people don't listen to each other's opinions, it's almost impossible to resolve disputes and reach agreements.

Interesting! And what about Voices of Youth?

Voices of Youth is the United Nations Children's Fund's (UNICEF's) digital community, on the U-Report website. Young campaigners aged 13–24 can share their own content, for example:

- personal stories
- poems
- fiction
- illustrations
- interviews
- photo essays

It's full of interesting content about the issues that matter to young people around the world – young people just like you.

But what if you don't know where to start with creating content?

Voices of Youth offers a lot of opportunities to learn. It has training videos that can help you to use your influence to make the world a better place. The advice from Voices of Youth enables you to create powerful campaign content such as blogs and videos, and to get other people to notice it.

Wow! That's fantastic! I can't wait to start.

B Underline these words in the text.

resolve   enables   representative   court   prevent   disputes

C Read and circle *True* or *False*.

1 Model United Nations copies the way that real UN groups discuss issues.   **True**   **False**

2 You have to travel to a different country to participate in Model United Nations.   **True**   **False**

3 Being in Model United Nations helps you understand that listening is a crucial skill for resolving disputes.   **True**   **False**

4 Voices of Youth is a website where children can learn about politicians' campaigns.   **True**   **False**

5 Voices of Youth videos can help you to organize a campaign.   **True**   **False**

D ⚙ Find the features in the text that help you answer these questions.

1 What three things can you learn from:

Model United Nations?   _______________________________

Voices of Youth?   _______________________________

2 What benefit did Elsa get from Model United Nations?

____

3 What did Jaden have to do for Model United Nations?

____

4 What artistic content do people share on Voices of Youth?

____

5 How does Mia want to make the world better?

____

Would you like to participate in Model United Nations? Why? / Why not?

A Match to make sentences.

1 An ambassador …
2 A park ranger …
3 A border guard …
4 A police officer …
5 A poacher …

a protects animals and their natural habitats.
b makes sure that people don't travel from one country to another illegally.
c is a hunter who isn't allowed to hunt in that place.
d is an important representative of a country or another organization.
e arrests people who are suspected of crimes.

B Read and complete the dialogues.

> border   illegal   poachers   arrest   park ranger   warn   steal   ambassador

Mrs. Evans: I'm fed up with people who ¹ ______________ things from my store. If they don't pay, my business loses money.

Jonas: Maybe you could put a sign on the door to ² ______________ people that you'll call the police about any crimes in your store. And if you put up some video cameras, the police will be able to identify and ³ ______________ anyone who does something ⁴ ______________ .

Luthando: Excuse me, are you a ⁵ ______________ ? Could I ask you how children like me can help you with your work at the park?

Mr. Nkosi: You could become a young ⁶ ______________ and tell people in your school about the importance of the wildlife here. But sorry, I can't talk about it now. I've just heard that some ⁷ ______________ have crossed the ⁸ ______________ at the edge of the park and are heading toward our rhinos. I have to stop them!

A Check (✓) the correct option.

1 Don't … on the wildflowers! All flowers are important!

☐ stamp   ☐ dictate

2 People often … Amelie's rude behavior.

☐ criticize   ☐ stamp

3 Simon wasn't our team leader, but he kept telling us what to do in a … way.

☐ calm down   ☐ bossy

4 They have no right to … how we live our lives!

☐ go on   ☐ dictate

5 Stop shouting! You need to … .

☐ calm down   ☐ criticize

B Read and complete the dialogue.

dictate   stamp   bossy   calm down   criticize

Mom: I can hear shouting. What's going on?

Minh: Bao said she was going to ¹ _______________ on my robot and break it!

Bao: That was because Minh said I had to stop playing my video game. She's so ² _______________ ! Why can't I just relax the way that I want?

Mom: ³ _______________ , both of you. Bao, you should never threaten to break people's things. That's not OK. But Minh, you can't ⁴ _______________ what Bao does all the time. And you shouldn't ⁵ _______________ her for playing a video game. She finished her homework and I said that she could play it.

A Read the persuasive letter. Label the different sections.

Purpose statement   Action statement   Date   Argument against   Closing
Recipient's address   Salutation   Signature   Conclusion   Argument for

---

____

____

____

____

____

____

____

____

____

Mrs. Erva Şahin
The Mayor
Meydan
375 Bankalar Cd. No: 88
68100 Aksaray

May 18

Dear Mrs. Şahin,

I'm writing to ask you to provide some Ping-Pong tables in the town park.

At the moment, it is hard for older children and teenagers to enjoy a visit to the park. There's a playground for younger children, and a café for adults. Unfortunately, these places aren't very suitable for us. I'm sure you will agree that this is not very fair. Luckily, there is a simple solution that will enable people of all ages to enjoy the park: outdoor Ping-Pong tables. We have some at our school, and they are always popular during recess. In addition, they will help us to develop better fitness and coordination.

Some people might say that there are more important things for the town to spend money on. However, what is more important than a fair and equal society? Also, outdoor Ping-Pong tables are very affordable compared with other solutions for entertaining older children.

If some Ping-Pong tables are provided in the park, I feel sure that they will benefit older children, and our town as a whole.

I hope you will support this suggestion.

Best regards,

Azra Önder

B Answer the questions.

1 What does Azra want? _______________________________________

2 What reasons does she give? _______________________________________

3 What reason against the idea does she include? _______________________________________

4 What persuasive language does she use? _______________________________________

C You're going to write a persuasive letter to someone important in your community. Think of something that you care about and brainstorm ideas. Use the graphic organizer to help you.

Who will I write to?	
What do I want to happen?	
Why is this important?	
How can I persuade the person I'm writing to?	

D Outline your ideas by completing the graphic organizer.

Why do I care about this?	
How can this situation improve in the future?	
What happens now? How do I know this?	

E Now write the first draft of your persuasive letter in your notebook. 

- Start your letter with a salutation and end it with a closing.
- Include language that will persuade the reader to agree with your arguments.
- In the first paragraph of your letter, clearly state your purpose for writing.
- Include a paragraph with arguments that support your point of view.
- Include a paragraph with at least one argument against your point of view.
- End your letter with an action statement that states what you want the reader to do.

F Check your work and make any necessary changes.

- Did you do everything in the list in **E**?
- Is your grammar, spelling, and punctuation correct?
- Is your writing clear and easy for other people to understand?

G Now write the final draft of your persuasive letter in your notebook. 

Student Book page 172

A Unscramble the words to complete the paragraph.

If you are an ¹ a_____________ (sdoasaambr), you live in a foreign country as your own country's ² r_____________ (rivateseptrene). To do the job well, you need good communication skills. If there is a ³ d_____________ (istedpu) between your country and the country where you are living, using the wrong words might turn the situation into a ⁴ c_____________ (risics). In the worst situations, ⁵ v_____________ (olvnciee) might start. However, if you can encourage people to ⁶ c_____________ _____________ (cmal dnwo) and look for peaceful ways to ⁷ r_____________ (lreveso) the problem, you can help to build a ⁸ l_____________ (nlog-etmr) friendly relationship between the two countries.

B Read and circle the correct option.

My aunt is a ¹ **park ranger** / **poacher** / **civilian** . It's her job to help protect the park and its wildlife. She has to be ² **bossy** / **illegal** / **long-term** and make sure people ³ **enable** / **stick to** / **steal** the rules. My aunt takes her job very seriously. She works extremely hard to ⁴ **criticize** / **prevent** / **border** the park and its wildlife from being harmed.

C Complete the conditional sentences with your own ideas.

1 If I could fly, ____ .

2 I'll be really happy if ____ .

3 If I study hard, ____ .

4 Water boils if ____ .

5 If I was famous, ____ .

Think and Reflect: Unit 15

My understanding of conflict ☆☆☆☆☆

How well I achieved my goal for Unit 15 ☆☆☆☆☆

The most interesting thing that I learned ____

My goal for Unit 16 ____

Vocabulary 1

A Read and complete the dialogues.

> cape   foam   hood   bang   bleed   pierce   cushion

1 **A:** What was that _______________ ?

   B: I think it was a firework.

2 **A:** It's cold outside! Don't forget your hat. And instead of a coat, you could wear your new _______________ .

   B: That has a _______________ , so I won't need a hat, too.

3 **A:** This _______________ 's very comfortable to sit on. What's it made of?

   B: I think it has _______________ inside.

4 **A:** Be careful with the needle, so you don't _______________ your skin as you sew.

   B: No, I don't want to _______________ onto the fabric!

B Circle the correct option.

1 She's a geologist, so rocks are her **specialty** / **steel**.

2 He's a fashion designer, so he's good at creating **gangs** / **outfits**.

3 I can't fold the plastic. It's too **steel** / **stiff**.

4 The knife and fork are made of **steel** / **specialty**.

5 The art masterpiece was stolen by a well-organized **gang** / **stiff**.

A Complete the sentences. Use each of these words twice.

> tear   wound   content   present

1 A _______________ rolled down her sad face.

2 You need to put a bandage on that _______________.

3 I bought you a _______________ to thank you for all your help.

4 She seems very _______________ in her new home. She really enjoys living there.

5 He _______________ the rope around the tree branch, then pulled.

6 Let's _______________ our ideas to everyone at the meeting.

7 I couldn't read the _______________ of the letter because of the bad handwriting.

8 There was a _______________ in my umbrella, so I got really wet.

B Check (✓) the sentences that use the third conditional.

1 ☐ If you had fallen, you would have hurt yourself.

2 ☐ I'd love to fly if I had superpowers.

3 ☐ Would they have come if they hadn't missed the bus?

4 ☐ I didn't notice that he had left the building.

5 ☐ We wouldn't have won the prize if we hadn't practiced so hard.

C Read and circle *Yes* or *No*.

1 If the superhero hadn't arrived in time to rescue them, the people would have been in danger.

Did the superhero arrive?   Yes   No

Were people in danger?   Yes   No

2 He would have fled if he'd seen a giant fox.

Did he see a giant fox?   Yes   No

Did he flee?   Yes   No

3 We wouldn't have refused to help if we hadn't been so busy.

Were we busy?   Yes   No

Did we refuse to help?   Yes   No

4 If I'd lost my bag, I would have had to pay for a new one.

Did I lose my bag?   Yes   No

Did I have to pay for a new one?   Yes   No

1 We were tired. We didn't walk to the waterfall.

   If we hadn't been tired, we would have walked to the waterfall.

2 Someone stole our car. We didn't drive home.

   ____

3 I forgot to do my chores. I wasn't allowed to watch TV.

   ____

4 He didn't use suncreen. He got sunburned.

   ____

5 It was dark. I didn't see the toy on the floor.

   ____

6 She didn't study for the test. She failed.

   ____

E **Read and complete the paragraph with the correct form of the verbs in parentheses. Use the third conditional.**

I've been reading a really exciting comic book recently. I love reading it, but it makes my room messy. Let me explain.
I [1] _______________________ (stop) reading my comic book earlier last night if it [2] _______________________ (not be) so exciting, and I [3] _______________________ (get) more sleep.
If I [4] _______________________ (not feel) so tired today,
I [5] _______________________ (be) more focused in my math lesson.
If I [6] _______________________ (concentrate) better in math, I [7] _______________________ (not make) so many mistakes. If I [8] _______________________ (not make) those mistakes, I [9] _______________________ (not have) extra homework this evening.
And if I [10] _______________________ (not be) so busy with homework,
I [11] _______________________ (clean) my room. But I didn't clean it, so now my room's a mess.

F **Complete the sentences for you.**

1 If I had grown up in a different country, ____ .

2 I would have been really annoyed if ____ .

3 I would have been really happy if ____ .

A ⚙ **Read the fantasy story. While you read, monitor your understanding. Read ahead and look at the pictures to help you clarify meaning. What does Su-Lin do to help her mother?**

Su-Lin and the Scubasuits

"How was your superhero work today, Mom?" Su-Lin asked Ace, who had just landed on the balcony.

"Professor Doom's gang have stolen a submarine and disappeared into the ocean!" Ace replied. "I have to find out what they're planning. Could you design me a new outfit to help me work underwater?"

Su-Lin started a sketch. An hour later, she showed Ace her scubasuit design.

"Weapons can't pierce the spider silk fabric, so you won't bleed underwater and attract sharks. And the helmet has a pointed shape made of waterproof foam, to help you move smoothly through the water. There's a steel oxygen tank on your back so you can breathe, and a powerful engine for high-speed travel. But you won't be invisible, so be careful the gang don't spot you!"

Ace had an idea. "They won't notice me if I'm really small. And making things bigger and smaller is your specialty, Su-Lin! Let's make two scubasuits, so you can come with me."

"No, Mom. I'm not a superhero," said Su-Lin. Then she thought some more. "It WOULD be interesting to try out my scubasuit design …"

A few days later, Ace and Su-Lin were speeding through the deep ocean in their new scubasuits. In the distance, they saw a glowing light.

"It must be Professor Doom's gang!" said Ace. "You know what to do now, Su-Lin!"

Su-Lin used her superpower to make herself and her mom the size of little fish. Then they moved closer to the gang to observe what was going on.

"Oh no! They're mining Marinotox!" cried Ace. "It's very valuable, but it could poison the ocean if it doesn't stay buried. We have to stop them!"

Su-Lin saw a strange-looking fish and had an idea. She made the fish much bigger, and Ace steered it toward the gang. When the gang saw the giant creature, they dropped their tools in fear and fled.

Next, Su-Lin swam down to the ocean floor. She used her pointed helmet to dig a little hole in the sand. Then she made the hole enormous. She watched as the Marinotox and the gang's tools and machines fell into the hole, and rocks and sand collapsed on top. Everything was safely buried.

"We did it!" said Ace. "If you hadn't come with me and used your superpower, I wouldn't have managed it. Thank you, Su-Lin!"

Su-Lin smiled. Maybe I am a superhero, she thought proudly.

B **Underline these words in the text.**

foam   pierce   specialty   steel   bleed   outfit

C **Read the story again and answer the questions.**

1 Why does Su-Lin mention sharks? _______________________________________

2 Why does Ace invite Su-Lin to come with her? ___________________________

3 Why does Su-Lin agree to go with Ace? _________________________________

4 What causes the glowing light? ____

5 Where does the creature that frightened the gang come from? ____________

6 Why does Su-Lin dig a little hole in the sand? __________________________

D **Read and circle *True* or *False*.**

1 Ace decides to look for Professor Doom's gang underwater because
   she knows what their plan is.   True   False

2 Su-Lin's scubasuit design makes people invisible.   True   False

3 People pay a lot of money for Marinotox.   True   False

4 Marinotox is only safe if you dig it up carefully.   True   False

5 The adventure makes Su-Lin feel differently about her identity. True   False

If you could be a superhero, what superpower would you choose?

A Circle the correct option.

1 There's a mailbox on a **rubber** / **post** outside our house.

2 You have to build the **sight** / **foundations** before you can build the walls.

3 A ball that's made of **rubber** / **marsh** bounces really high.

4 You should wear boots if you want to walk in the **post** / **marsh**.

5 The rain has been **still** / **wearing away** the statue's face.

6 I want to go to Rome and see the famous **sights** / **wear away**.

B Complete the second sentence so its meaning is similar to the first one.

> still   worn away   marsh   in contact with   sight

1 Don't move! → Stay _______________!

2 The Eiffel Tower is France's most famous landmark. → The Eiffel Tower is France's most famous _______________.

3 Did your hand touch the fire? → Did your hand come _______________ the fire?

4 Over the years, the middle of the step has become lower because of people's feet walking on it. → Over the years, the middle of the step has been _______________ by people's feet.

5 The wetland is the home of thousands of birds. → The _______________ is the home of thousands of birds.

A **Circle the correct option.**

1 Let's hang the tire from a branch with a **rope** / **wire**.

2 A lot of clothes are made from cotton **cable** / **fiber**.

3 The butterfly picture has been drawn with a line that's **continuous** / **cable**.

4 To prevent people from climbing the fence, they've put across some **wire** / **loop**.

5 The electricity travels around the building along long, thick **continuous** / **cables**.

6 The scariest part of our roller coaster ride was when we went round the **loop** / **rope**.

B **Read and circle *True* or *False*.**

1 A wire is usually thicker than a cable.	**True**	**False**
2 A cable can help us lift extremely heavy objects.	**True**	**False**
3 Something continuous stops regularly.	**True**	**False**
4 A loop goes round in a circle shape.	**True**	**False**
5 Fiber for making fabric comes from both plants and animals.	**True**	**False**
6 A rope can help us climb rocks and cliffs.	**True**	**False**

16 Writing Study

A Underline the prepositional phrases of place in the sentences.

1 I love trips in cable cars.

2 He was walking on top of the Great Wall of China.

3 They used the parking lot outside the train station.

4 The bridge couldn't have heavy trucks on it.

5 There is a lot of mud beneath the buildings of Venice.

6 There was a secret tunnel behind the painting.

B Unscramble the sentences.

1 the bench / on / put / She / some comfortable cushions

____

2 around / a circle of stones / Someone / the fire / had placed

____

3 a lot of buildings / destroyed / the city / in / The earthquake

____

4 next to / They / the castle / built / a river

____

5 a new restaurant / the flower store / I / spotted / opposite

____

C Write a paragraph about a visit to a famous building. Use prepositional phrases of place.

Last year, my class went to the Red Fort in Delhi. It's a huge place, with high, thick walls of red stone around a central area of gardens. We entered the fort at the Lahori Gate and saw a busy market in front of us. There was an interesting roof above the market. But my favorite part of the fort was the Delhi Gate, where two stone elephant statues stand opposite each other. I also loved the flower decorations on the walls.

____

____

____

____

____

A **Read and circle the correct option.**

Last semester, I was in a play. I enjoyed the acting, but I hated my costume. I had a long red [1] **post / cape / marsh** that was kept on my shoulders by a [2] **rubber / hood / loop** of string. One time I tripped over the long fabric and got a [3] **fiber / bang / wire** on my head when I fell down. I had to wear a heavy [4] **steel / cable / sight** mask that was really uncomfortable. Also, I had a [5] **continuous / still / stiff** leather jacket that rubbed my neck so much that it [6] **wore away / bang / gang** some skin and made me [7] **cushion / pierce / bleed**. I was so happy taking off that [8] **rope / outfit / specialty** for the last time!

B **Unscramble the words to complete the sentences.**

1 Boots made of r_____________ (brbure) are useful, because they're waterproof.

2 Make sure you don't let the cleaning product come in c_____________ _____________ (toccnat tihw) your eyes.

3 She tied the dog to a p_____________ (sopt) so it couldn't run away.

4 Deep f_____________ (uonsinfodat) will help to keep the building stable.

C **Complete the third conditional sentences with the correct form of the verbs.**

> not use   bring   not overhear   not have to   break

1 We wouldn't have gotten lost if we _____________________ a map.

2 If I hadn't been near the door, I _____________________ their conversation.

3 They would have defeated her if she _____________________ her superpowers.

4 The cable car's cable _____________________ if they had attached another cabin to it.

5 If we _____________________ lie on the floor, we would have slept better.

Think and Reflect: Unit 16

My understanding of strength ☆☆☆☆☆

How well I achieved my goal for Unit 16 ☆☆☆☆☆

The most interesting thing that I learned _____________________

My goal for Unit 17 _____________________

17 How can we keep our bodies strong?

Vocabulary 1

A **Match the sentences with the pictures.**

1 I always start the day with some cereal.

2 Let's make a pasta sauce with this ground beef.

3 You can buy a wide variety of dairy products.

4 Many vegetarian dishes contain lentils.

5 Do you know where this salmon was caught?

6 I love to put canned tuna in my sandwiches.

a

b

c

d

e

f

B **Read and circle *True* or *False*.**

1 The adults who you live with should never know what you're up to. True False
2 Your heart beats constantly. True False
3 A picky eater is happy to eat all types of food. True False
4 You have nails on your knees and your wrists. True False
5 Oxygen, water, and food are essential for your body. True False
6 The entire surface of the planet is covered in water. True False

A **Read and complete the paragraphs.**

> guitar   yogurt   etc.   kindergarten   shampoo   broccoli   orchestra   restaurant

We had a meal at a [1] ________________ last night, but it wasn't very nice. I ate lamb with some vegetables: carrots and [2] ________________ . It had a white sauce made of [3] ________________ and herbs, but unfortunately it tasted like the [4] ________________ that I put on my hair!

I've always loved playing music. When I was in [5] ________________ , I liked playing rhythms on drums, whistles, [6] ________________ . These days, I'm learning to play the [7] ________________ . I'm going to join my school's [8] ________________ when I can play well enough.

B **Read and circle the correct option.**

1 She's talking about the **past** / **present** .
She **lives** / **doesn't live** in the mountains now.

2 They **arrived** / **didn't arrive** late.
He's **happy** / **sad** about the time that they arrived.

3 He **can** / **can't** run fast.
He **wants** / **doesn't want** the situation to be different.

4 She's talking about the **past** / **present** .
She **remembered** / **didn't remember** her lunch.

C **Check (✓) the correct option.**

1 I wish I … have to do homework now.

☐ don't   ☐ didn't

2 If only she … make so much noise every day!

☐ doesn't   ☐ didn't

3 I wish I … put on my coat this morning.

☐ had   ☐ was

4 I wish I … lost my pencil case yesterday.

☐ didn't   ☐ hadn't

5 If only there … more science-fiction books in the library today.

☐ were   ☐ are

6 If only I … the competition, but I didn't. Tamsin won as usual.

☐ 'd won   ☐ won

D **Complete the sentences. Use the correct form of the verbs in parentheses.**

1 I wish my parents _______________ more patient in the mornings. (be)

2 If only it _______________ last night! (not snow)

3 If only I _______________ more time to relax these days! (have)

4 I wish I _______________ learning the piano when I was younger. (start)

5 If only my chores _______________ so long every evening. (not take)

6 I wish I _______________ my neighbor's window yesterday. (not break)

E **Complete the sentences. Use the correct form of the verbs in parentheses.**

1 I went to bed late and now I'm tired. (go)

I wish I hadn't gone to bed so late.

2 I've just moved to Spain but I can't speak Spanish. (speak)

If only ____

3 I didn't brush my teeth regularly and now I have a cavity. (brush)

I wish ____

4 I dropped the dessert and now no one can eat it. (drop)

If only ____

5 I'm short so I can't reach the cookies. (be)

If only ____

6 I don't own a bike so I have to walk to school. (own)

I wish ____

What three wishes would you like to make?

Smithside Elementary School Blog

Tuesday, June 26

Class feast

We decided to start this week with a class feast. On the weekend, the children used what they had learned from nutritionist Miguel Ramos to create a healthy dish at home. Then, on Monday afternoon, the school's microwave oven was very busy as we heated up the results. What a wonderful meal we had!

Today, we've been recording the recipes. Here are two of our favorites.

Seedy salmon with stir-fried vegetables

I knew from last week's learning that salmon, seeds, and vegetables all have a lot of essential nutrients. This recipe combines all three, and it's delicious. Cora

4 pieces of salmon

salt and pepper

75g mixed seeds

carrots, red or yellow peppers, and broccoli, cut into thin sticks

garlic, chopped into tiny pieces

vegetable oil

lime juice

1 Put a little salt and pepper on the salmon pieces.

2 Place the seeds on a plate and push the salmon pieces onto them, so the entire surface is covered in seeds.

3 Bake the salmon in the oven at 220°C for about 15 minutes, until all the flesh is pale pink. Remove from the oven.

4 Fry the vegetable sticks in oil, stirring constantly.

5 After two minutes, add the garlic, and fry for two more minutes.

6 Add some lime juice, and eat with the salmon.

Pasta with lentil bolognese

I'm trying to eat less red meat, so I decided to make my favorite pasta sauce with lentils instead of ground beef. It tasted great. If only I'd made a larger quantity so I could store some in the freezer! Ali

1 onion	400g canned chopped tomatoes	juice of 1 lemon
1 carrot	200g brown lentils	50g tomato paste
100g mushrooms	1 vegetable stock cube	salt and pepper
olive oil	1 teaspoon dried mixed herbs	350g dried pasta

1 Chop all the fresh vegetables into small pieces.

2 Fry the fresh vegetables with olive oil, salt, and pepper for about 15 minutes, stirring occasionally.

3 When the vegetables are soft, add the tomatoes, lentils, stock cube, herbs, lemon juice, and tomato paste. Cook on a low heat for about 30 minutes.

4 Cook the pasta, and eat it with the pasta sauce on top. If you eat dairy products, you might like to stir in some cheese.

B **Underline these words in the text.**

ground beef   essential   constantly   dairy products   entire

C **Scan the blog and find this information.**

1 the date that the blog post was published

2 how they heated up the food at school

3 the name of the student that cooked seedy salmon

4 what shape to cut the vegetables for the stir-fry

5 how long to cook the bolognese after the lentils have been added

D **Check (✓) the correct answer.**

1 Whose recipe uses lime?

☐ Cora's   ☐ Ali's

2 What do you have to stir constantly?

☐ stir-fried vegetables   ☐ bolognese sauce

3 What would Ali like to do with his recipe?

☐ make it with ground beef   ☐ freeze some of it

4 How do you know when to stop cooking the seedy salmon?

☐ by the color of the flesh   ☐ by the color of the seeds

5 Which person chose a recipe because it includes a lot of important nutrients?

☐ Cora   ☐ Ali

A **Cross out and replace one incorrect word in these sentences. Don't change the underlined words.**

1 Your <u>abdominal muscles</u> are behind your <u>stomach</u>. ___________

2 Your <u>thigh</u> is the part of your <u>leg</u> below your <u>knee</u>. ___________

3 Your food flows through <u>tubes</u> inside your <u>body</u> named <u>blood vessels</u>. ___________

4 We get cold when we do <u>aerobic exercise</u>. ___________

5 Some adults lift weights to <u>strengthen</u> their eyes. ___________

6 A <u>personal trainer</u> helps <u>people</u> to forget their <u>fitness</u>. ___________

B **Complete the sentences.**

stretch   thighs   blood vessels   personal trainer   abdominal   aerobic exercise

1 Rubber is a useful material because you can _______________ it.

2 This exercise is good for your _______________ muscles.

3 His shorts cover his _______________.

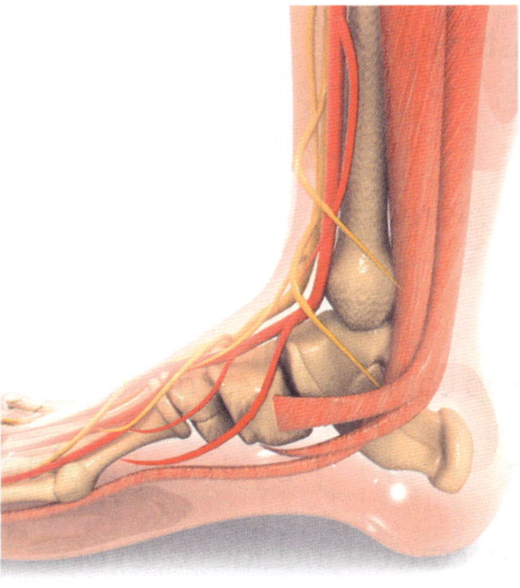

4 Victoria loves her job as a _______________.

5 This image shows the _______________ in a foot.

6 People usually sweat when they do _______________.

A **Check (✓) the correct option.**

1 I had a flu … yesterday.

☐ sum up　　☐ vaccination　　☐ immune system

2 I used to get a lot of infections. But now I take a special medication that strengthens my ….

☐ sum up　　☐ vaccination　　☐ immune system

3 To … my presentation, we need to eat well, sleep well, and exercise.

☐ vaccination　　☐ effectively　　☐ sum up

4 I waste a lot of time when I study. I wish I could study more ….

☐ clarify　　☐ effectively　　☐ substance

5 I don't understand. Please can you … what you mean?

☐ clarify　　☐ effectively　　☐ substance

6 There was a disgusting black … on the window, so I cleaned it.

☐ substance　　☐ clarify　　☐ effectively

B **Read and complete the paragraph.**

> clarify　immune system　effectively
> vaccination　sum up　substance

Let's [1] _______________ the main things that we've learned today. First, we learned that our [2] _______________ tries to stop us getting ill. It can do this more [3] _______________ if we make healthy choices about how we live. We also learned that when we have a [4] _______________, a doctor or nurse puts a [5] _______________, usually a liquid, inside us to make our body better at fighting a particular disease. Now, does anyone have any questions? I'll try to [6] _______________ anything that you're confused about.

A **Underline the reporting verbs in the dialogue.**

"Let's go swimming!" suggested Mo.

"That's a good idea," agreed Maryam.

"I can take you to the swimming pool this afternoon," offered Dad.

"Thanks, Dad," said Mo, "but can't we go on our own?"

"A lot of our friends go without their parents these days," explained Maryam. "They take the bus."

"I'm sorry, children. I would worry about you too much," admitted Dad.

"Oh, Dad, please!" begged the children.

B **Check (✓) the correct option.**

1 "Please, please, please can I stay up late tonight?" ….

☐ begged Lena ☐ agreed Lena ☐ Lena agreed

2 "I don't lift weights because I'm scared of dropping one on my foot," ….

☐ he suggested ☐ admitted he ☐ he admitted

3 "Hey! Why don't we make something with lentils?" ….

☐ Jemal suggested ☐ Jemal explained ☐ explained Jemal

4 "I'll lend you my boots if you want," ….

☐ Saeed admitted ☐ admitted Saeed ☐ offered Saeed

C **Write a paragraph from a story about doing a healthy activity. Include dialogue with a variety of reporting verbs.**

"Let's go mountain biking today," suggested Pip.

"I don't know," replied Annabel doubtfully. "I don't have my own bike. I can ride a bike, but I've never ridden anywhere except regular roads."

"You can borrow my brother's," offered Pip. "I'm sure you'd enjoy mountain biking if you tried it. It's really exciting!'

"OK, I'll give it a try," agreed Annabel.

____

____

____

____

A **Read and circle the correct option.**

An experienced [1] **blood vessel / personal trainer / immune system** can help you to find types of [2] **substance / nail / aerobic exercise** that you enjoy, and to use your exercise time as [3] **effectively / picky / constantly** as possible. They can give you the motivation to [4] **clarify / sum up / lift weights** or do other exercises to [5] **strengthen / be up to / ground beef** your muscles, and remind you to [6] **salmon / stretch / tuna** your muscles before and after your workouts.

B **Unscramble the words to complete the dialogue.**

Pablo: Hi, Dad! I'm inventing a new, healthy breakfast [1] c_____________ (lereca). I've put all my favorite ingredients in: rolled wheat, seeds, and dried fruit.

Dad: That sounds good for a [2] p_____________ (ikypc) eater like you. But isn't your favorite food [3] t_____________ (utan)? Why not throw some of that in, too?!

Pablo: Oh, that's not a bad idea! Oily fish is really good for your heart, your [4] i_____________ s_____________ (nemimu semsty), and your hair and [5] n_____________ (ilnas). It sounds weird, but I'll give it a try!

C **Complete the second sentences. Use a verb from the first sentence.**

1 It rained all day.

I wish _it hadn't rained all day_____________ .

2 I stayed up late last night.

If only _____________________________ .

3 I have an allergy to chocolate.

I wish _____________________________ .

4 I can't afford to buy those sneakers.

I wish _____________________________ .

5 I have an uncomfortable bed.

If only _____________________________ .

6 I didn't remember my aunt's birthday.

I wish _____________________________ .

Think and Reflect: Unit 17

My understanding of strength ☆☆☆☆☆

How well I achieved my goal for Unit 17 ☆☆☆☆☆

The most interesting thing that I learned _________________________________

My goal for Unit 18 _________________________________

18 What can our mental strength help us to do?

Vocabulary 1

A Read and complete the dialogue.

> dull   steadily   depressing   shift   determination   welcoming   bazaar   ran into

Pola: Hi, Jakub. Did you have a good weekend?

Jakub: It wasn't terrible, but it was a little ¹ ________________ . It's hard to have fun when it's raining all the time. But one interesting thing happened: I ² ________________ Natalia in town!

Pola: Really? I haven't seen her since she moved house. How is she?

Jakub: Fine. It was ³ ________________ for her at first, because all her friends lived so far away and the children in her new class weren't very ⁴ ________________ . But she's ⁵ ________________ making new friends now. How was your weekend?

Pola: Good, thanks. I was helping my music group to organize a ⁶ ________________ . I did a four-hour ⁷ ________________ , and it was tiring but fun. It has taken a lot of ⁸ ________________ to raise the funds that we need for new instruments, and it feels great that we've finally managed it.

B Read and circle the correct option.

Fundraising Tips: Organizing a Bazaar

1 Plan carefully so that the bazaar can **go ahead** / **let you down** even if there's bad weather.

2 **Recruit** / **Display** the most interesting objects where customers are most likely to notice them.

3 **Recruit** / **Run into** tons of volunteers, so people don't have to work very long **shifts** / **determination** at the bazaar.

4 Keep a list of extra volunteers who you can contact if someone **displays** / **lets you down** on the day.

5 Encourage your volunteers to give customers a **welcoming** / **depressing** smile. People might spend more money if the volunteers are friendly.

6 Remember that organizing a bazaar isn't easy, but with **shift** / **determination** and hard work, you'll succeed!

Word Study and Grammar

A **Complete the sentences with these prepositions. Use some of the words twice.**

> on   for   with   about   in

1 I've succeeded _______________ raising the money for a new Ping-Pong table.

2 They congratulated us _______________ our victory in the game.

3 Who's going to pay _______________ your new sneakers, you or your parents?

4 I feel really bad, because I forgot _______________ my grandma's birthday.

5 Please don't involve me _______________ your argument.

6 I shared the cake _______________ my family, and it was absolutely delicious!

7 Please thank Marisol _______________ all her help.

8 Have they decided _______________ the baby's name yet?

B **Match the sentences with the tenses.**

1 She's been reading. •   • **a** simple present

2 They weren't listening. •   • **b** present continuous

3 I speak English. •   • **c** simple past

4 Have you seen that movie? •   • **d** past continuous

5 We're coming. •   • **e** present perfect

6 He hadn't been there before. •   • **f** present perfect continuous

7 Did we visit them yesterday? •   • **g** past perfect

C **Check (✓) the correct option.**

1 What … for breakfast every morning?

   ☐ do you eat   ☐ had you eaten

2 One day last year, I … a big spider in my shoe.

   ☐ have been finding   ☐ found

3 What … at eight o'clock last night?

   ☐ has he been doing   ☐ was he doing

4 I … my homework yet.

   ☐ haven't done   ☐ wasn't doing

5 Why … on the floor right now?

   ☐ are you sitting   ☐ do you sit

 Correct the mistakes in the underlined verbs.

1 My brother <u>play</u> baseball every Monday. _______________

2 <u>We going</u> on a hike next weekend. _______________

3 They <u>didn't sang</u> in yesterday's concert. _______________

4 We <u>was waiting</u> outside the café. _______________

5 I <u>haven't being laughing</u> at you. _______________

E **Complete the sentences. Use the correct form of the verbs in parentheses.**

1 _______________ (you, work) at the bazaar all day? You must be tired!

2 Two hours ago, I _______________ (break) my dad's computer screen.

3 I _______________ (hang out) in the park when I ran into my friend Nico.

4 So far this year, I _______________ (visit) the hospital three times.

5 My parents _______________ (not go) to bed early. They're usually still awake at 11:00 p.m.

6 _______________ (she, have) any other jobs before she became an astronaut?

F **Answer the questions for you.**

1 What did you do last Sunday? _______________

2 What were you doing before you went to bed yesterday? _______________

3 What interesting things have you done this year? _______________

4 When were you last late for something? Why? _______________

Did you remember all these tenses? Which ones do you use regularly?

A **Read the story. How, eventually, did the children learn first aid?**

A Thirst for First Aid

Aya and Mariam saw the news headline: *Boy saves father's life with first aid skills.*

"Wow! That's impressive!" said Aya. "I've never learned any first aid."

"I haven't, either," said Mariam. "I'd really let my parents down if they needed me to save them. Maybe we should do something about it!"

The next day, the girls asked their teacher, Madam Ibrahim, if she could teach them some first aid in class, but Madam Ibrahim said there wasn't time for that during the school day. They also researched after-school first aid clubs, but unfortunately the nearest club was too far away.

They were disappointed, but determined not to give up. "Maybe we can learn from online videos," suggested Mariam.

The next two Saturdays, the two girls went to Mariam's house and tried to learn first aid skills from videos. But they weren't sure if they were doing things right, and there was no one to ask. "This is depressing," sighed Mariam. "We've been trying for hours, but we aren't learning much."

"Maybe we could ask a doctor to teach us," suggested Aya.

They wrote to their local doctor, Dr. Mahmoud, who soon replied:

From: Dr. Mahmoud

I'm afraid I work long shifts and don't have enough time to teach you. But I'll discuss this issue with the Health Council. Hopefully we can come up with a solution.

Two months later, Madam Ibrahim made an announcement in class.

"There's going to be a new after-school club in the town hall, and I think some of you will be really interested." She smiled at Mariam and Aya. "It's a first aid club!"

Dr. Mahmoud had persuaded the Health Council to recruit a first aid teacher, Mr. Saad. Aya, Mariam, and thirteen other children went excitedly to the first session, and it was fantastic! Mr. Saad showed them how to roll someone into a safe lying position. Then he said, "Go ahead and practice with your partner." He watched them carefully and helped them to get it exactly right.

Their skills improved steadily each week, and soon they were ready to take part in a first aid competition against other clubs. As they were heading to the competition by bus, a passenger suddenly fell to the floor.

"Oh no! How can we help?" the adults nearby said in confusion. But the children looked at each other confidently. They knew exactly what to do!

B **Underline these words in the text.**

shifts   depressing   go ahead   recruit   let my parents down   steadily

C **Write the letters a–f to show the chain reaction of cause and effect.**

1 [e] → 2 [ ] → 3 [ ] → 4 [ ] → 5 [ ] → 6 [ ] → 7 [ ]

a They wrote to a doctor to ask him to teach them.

b They realized that other people's lives might one day be in danger because of their lack of first aid skills.

c The doctor persuaded the Health Council to recruit a first aid teacher.

d They wanted a way to learn first aid.

e Mariam and Aya saw a headline about someone using first aid skills to save a life.

f When there was an emergency on the bus, they knew what to do.

g Children learned first aid skills from the first aid teacher.

D **Complete the sentences.**

1 ________________ and ________________ didn't have time to teach the girls first aid.

2 The girls couldn't go to the nearest first aid club that they'd found out about, because it ________________________ .

3 Learning first aid from online videos was hard for the girls, because they didn't know if ________________________ .

4 In their first session at the first aid club, they learned ________________________ .

5 The children were on a bus because ________________________ .

6 When there was a health emergency on the bus, the ________________________ didn't know what to do.

A Complete the sentences.

> left out   bravery   episode   amazed   chest   authentically   unpleasant   remarkable

1 I'm ________________ that she ran the race so quickly. No one has ever run it so fast! It really was a ________________ achievement.

2 All my friends went to Amelia's house on the weekend to watch the latest ________________ of our favorite TV show. But no one invited me, so I felt ________________.

3 He spoke ________________ about his experiences. It took a lot of ________________ to be so honest about what had happened.

4 He breathed in the polluted air, and immediately had an ________________ feeling in his ________________.

B Read and circle *True* or *False*.

1 Your lungs and heart are in your chest. True False

2 When something dull happens, people are always amazed. True False

3 Doing things that scare you shows your bravery. True False

4 On TV, a story is often divided into several episodes. True False

5 It's fun to feel left out. True False

6 People enjoy doing things that are unpleasant. True False

A Check (✓) the correct option.

1 If your teeth hurt, you should … with your dentist and arrange a checkup.

☐ get in touch   ☐ forgive

2 I really … in the soccer game. We lost because of my mistake.

☐ blamed   ☐ messed up

3 I broke my brother's camera. Do you think he'll ever … me?

☐ forgive   ☐ mess up

4 I'm not very good at art, but … I'm pretty musical.

☐ at least   ☐ get in touch

5 I enjoy doing papier mâché …, but it isn't one of my regular hobbies.

☐ at least   ☐ from time to time

6 Don't … your sister for making us late. You weren't ready for school either.

☐ from time to time   ☐ blame

B Read and complete the paragraph.

> got in touch   messed up   at least   blamed   forgave   from time to time

My friend Daniela moved to a different city last year.
I really miss her, but ¹ _______________________
she doesn't live too far away, so we can still see each
other ² _______________________ . Last month, she
³ _______________________ to invite me to a theme
park. I was really excited to go, but unfortunately,
I ⁴ _______________________ . The day before
our trip, I realized that it was the same day as a
kayaking day that my parents had arranged. I had
to abandon our theme park plan. At first, Daniela
⁵ _______________________ me for ruining the
plan, but she soon ⁶ _______________________
me. I hope we'll be able to go to the theme park
together another time.

A **Read the biography. Label the different sections.**

Main achievements   Conclusion   Childhood   Introduction   Becoming successful

Rafael Nadal

Rafael Nadal is a tennis player from Spain, and one of the greatest tennis champions in history.

He was born on the Spanish island of Mallorca. One of his uncles was a soccer player for the Spanish national team, and, as a boy, Rafael showed a lot of interest in this sport. However, another uncle, Toni, had been a tennis player. Toni introduced Rafael to tennis when he was only three, and noticed his talent immediately. By the time Rafael was five, he was getting regular training from Toni.

Rafael became Spanish junior tennis champion at the age of 11. After he won his first international competition the next year, he decided to give up soccer and focus all his energy on school work and tennis. As a 14-year-old, he broke a finger in an important game, but he gripped his racket with the other fingers and won both the game and the competition. However, his bravery wasn't as clear in other areas of his life. Training with his uncle often made him cry, and he was afraid of deep water, dogs, and the dark. Luckily, his incredible determination overcame these challenges.

Since then, he has won all of the world's most important tennis competitions more than once, and he has two Olympic gold medals. He's also won prizes for being a good sport. He has set up a sports charity for disadvantaged children, and he has given generous support to many other charities.

His success in sport and his kind, calm attitude have inspired many people. He is a hero both on and off the tennis court.

B **Answer the questions.**

1 Which tenses are used to talk about Nadal's childhood and teenage years?

____

2 Which tense is used for Nadal's main achievements?

____

3 What phrases does the writer use to tell us Nadal's age when different things happened?

____

4 What does the biography reveal about Nadal's personality?

____

C **You're going to write a biography. Choose a person who's still alive and brainstorm ideas. Use the graphic organizer to help you.**

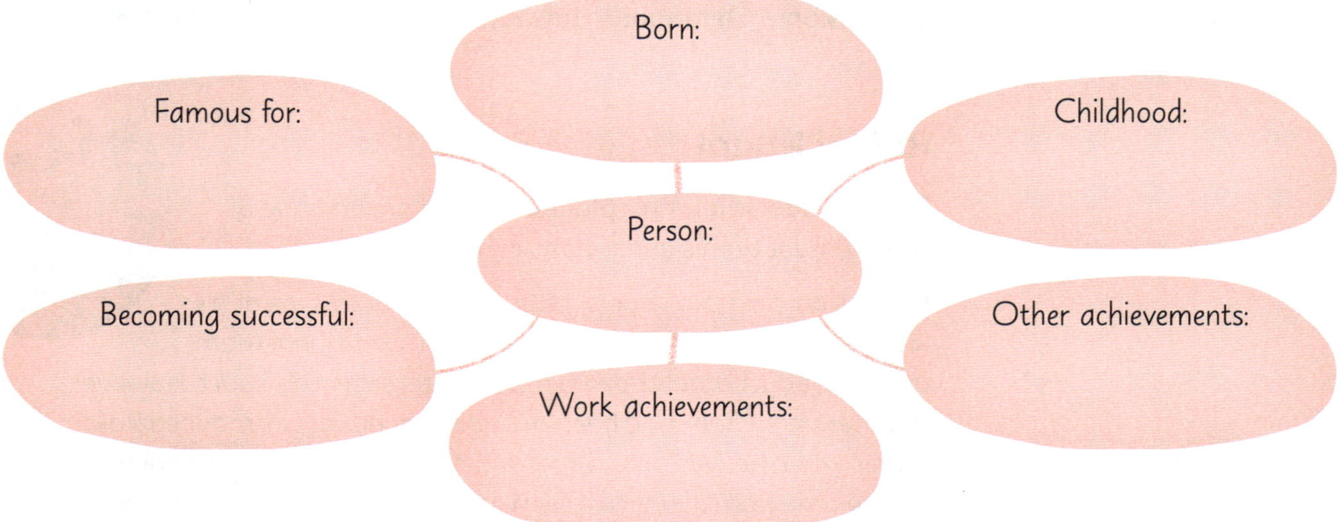

D **Outline your ideas by completing the chart.**

Introduction:

Childhood:

Becoming successful:

Main achievements:

Conclusion:

E **Now write the first draft of your biography in your notebook.** 

- Include the achievements that have made the person famous.
- Talk about any challenges that they have overcome.
- Include things that they have done that reveal their personality.
- Say why the person is special.
- Use expressions to show the passing of time.

F **Check your work and make any necessary changes.**

- Did you do everything in the list in **E**?
- Is your grammar, spelling, and punctuation correct?
- Is your writing clear and easy for other people to understand?

G **Now write the final draft of your biography in your notebook.**

A **Unscramble the words to complete the sentences.**

1 What's that u______________ (p e u t n n l a s a) smell? Oh no! The food's burning! I'm sorry, I've l______________ (e t l) you d______________ (o d n w) with the cooking again.

2 It isn't fair to b______________ (l m e b a) her. She tried very hard and didn't want to m______________ ______________ (e s s m   p u), and it wasn't a bad mistake, either.

B **Read and circle the correct option.**

[1] **From time to time** / **At least**, I go to a [2] **bazaar** / **chest** with my family. We love looking for nice things to buy there, and the sellers are usually very [3] **left out** / **welcoming**. I'm always [4] **amazed** / **depressing** that other people prefer buying things from ordinary stores. Most of the stores in my town sell the same things for years, so visiting them is very [5] **dull** / **remarkable**.

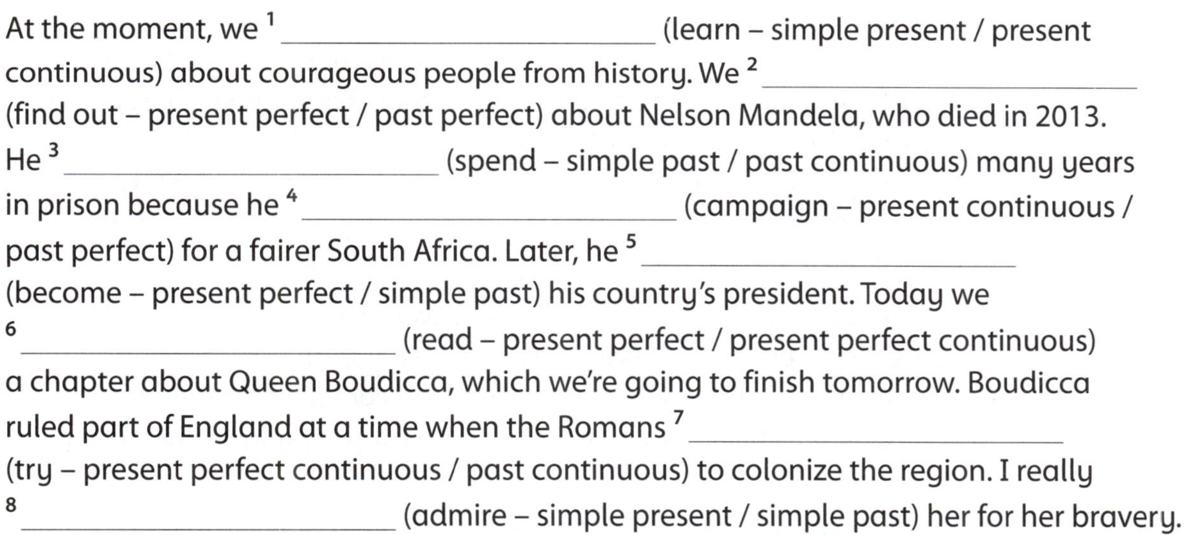

C **Complete the sentences with the correct form of the verbs in parentheses. Use one of the tenses given.**

At the moment, we [1] ______________________ (learn – simple present / present continuous) about courageous people from history. We [2] ______________________ (find out – present perfect / past perfect) about Nelson Mandela, who died in 2013. He [3] ______________________ (spend – simple past / past continuous) many years in prison because he [4] ______________________ (campaign – present continuous / past perfect) for a fairer South Africa. Later, he [5] ______________________ (become – present perfect / simple past) his country's president. Today we [6] ______________________ (read – present perfect / present perfect continuous) a chapter about Queen Boudicca, which we're going to finish tomorrow. Boudicca ruled part of England at a time when the Romans [7] ______________________ (try – present perfect continuous / past continuous) to colonize the region. I really [8] ______________________ (admire – simple present / simple past) her for her bravery.

Think and Reflect: Unit 18

My understanding of strength ☆☆☆☆☆

How well I achieved my goal for Unit 18 ☆☆☆☆☆

The most interesting thing that I learned ______________________

News Report

A **Read the news report. Label the different sections.**

Byline   Extra details and quotes   Closing   Lead   Headline

School Sports Day is a Massive Success!

By our reporter, Pete Burkall   June 25

On Saturday, in the beautiful sports field at Northgate Primary School, a big crowd of excited students gathered for the school's annual sports day. They were joined by all their teachers and many proud parents. Every year this event celebrates physical activity, teamwork, and sportsmanship. There was a variety of activities for the students. The atmosphere this year was fantastic and the sun kept shining all day long!

Parents and teachers waved and cheered enthusiastically as the students participated in each activity. The students from Grades 1 and 2 started the sports day with a tug-of-war that was great fun to watch! Next up was a 100-meter sprint race for Grades 3 and 4. Grade 3 winner, Ben Mattis, achieved a personal best. Afterward, he told me: "It wasn't about winning for me. I had tons of fun competing with my classmates!"

A group of six students from Grade 5 were chosen to help organize the whole event. Mr. Chan, the head of sports at Northgate Primary, explained: "Our students spent the day setting up activities, making sure all the children had plenty of water, and explaining the rules of each activity."

Julieta from Grade 5 said, "It was a chance for me to practice my leadership skills, and to learn how to organize and run an event!"

Northgate Primary School's sports day was an incredible success. It provided an exciting opportunity for students to create happy memories. I can't wait to report on next year's event!

B **Answer the questions.**

1   Who is the writer? ____

2   What, where, and when was the event? _______________________________

3   Who did the writer interview for the report? ___________________________

4   How does the writer close the article about the event? ___________________

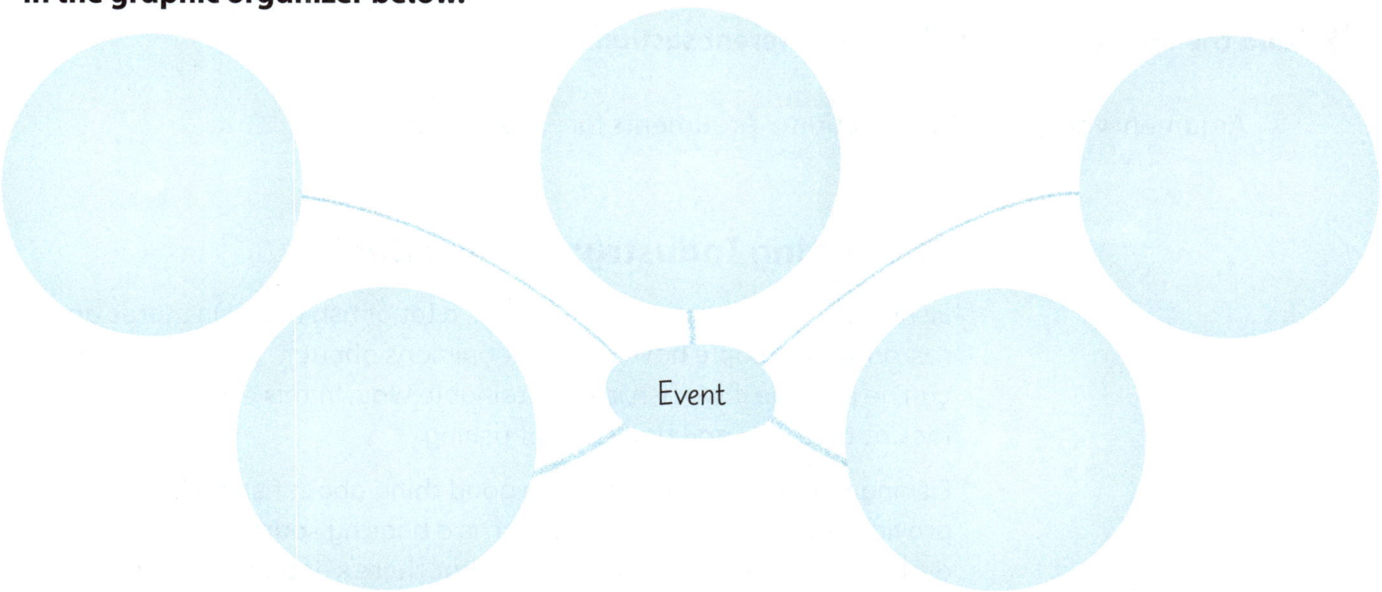

D **Outline your ideas by completing the chart.**

Headline:

Byline:

Lead:

Extra details and quotes:

Closing:

E **Now write the first draft of your news report in your notebook.** 

- Start your news report with a headline and remember to include the byline.
- Say what and where the event was, and who took part.
- Add extra details and quotes.
- Close your article with a final statement or thought.

F **Check your work and make any necessary changes.**

- Did you do everything in the list in **E**?
- Is your grammar, spelling, and punctuation correct?
- Is your writing clear and easy for other people to understand?

G **Now write the final draft of your news report in your notebook.** 

Opinion Essay

A **Read the opinion essay. Label the different sections.**

Arguments against   Introduction   Arguments for   Conclusion

The Fishing Industry: Good or Bad?

Fishing is a big industry that provides a lot of fish to sell in stores and restaurants. People have different opinions about it, but I think fishing can be positive if we fish in a sustainable way. In this essay, we will look at the good and bad sides of fishing.

Fishing has several benefits. One good thing about fishing is that it provides food for many people. Fish is a healthy source of protein and other nutrients. Fishing means that there's enough fish for everyone to eat. Fishing also creates jobs for fishers and workers in fish processing factories. That work helps families and communities because it provides money that they can use for their everyday lives.

However, there are also some negative things. One problem is overfishing. Often, too many fish are caught. This leads to some types of fish becoming endangered or even extinct. Another issue is bycatch. This is when other animals, such as turtles and seabirds, get caught in nets by mistake. Finally, fishing impacts on the pollution of our oceans. Nets and other fishing equipment are lost or thrown away, and wildlife can get injured because of this.

In conclusion, the fishing industry has important benefits, but it also has negative points. In my opinion, we cannot provide enough food for the world's population unless the fishing industry continues, but we need stronger laws to stop its negative impacts. As long as fishing becomes more sustainable, I believe that it can be good for the world.

B **Answer the questions.**

1   How does the writer begin the essay?

____

2   What positive and negative points does the writer make?

Positive: ____

Negative: ____

3   Which paragraphs begin with a topic sentence that tells the reader the main idea of the paragraph?

____

4   How does the writer end the essay?

C You're going to write an opinion essay. Brainstorm. Write your ideas in the graphic organizer below.

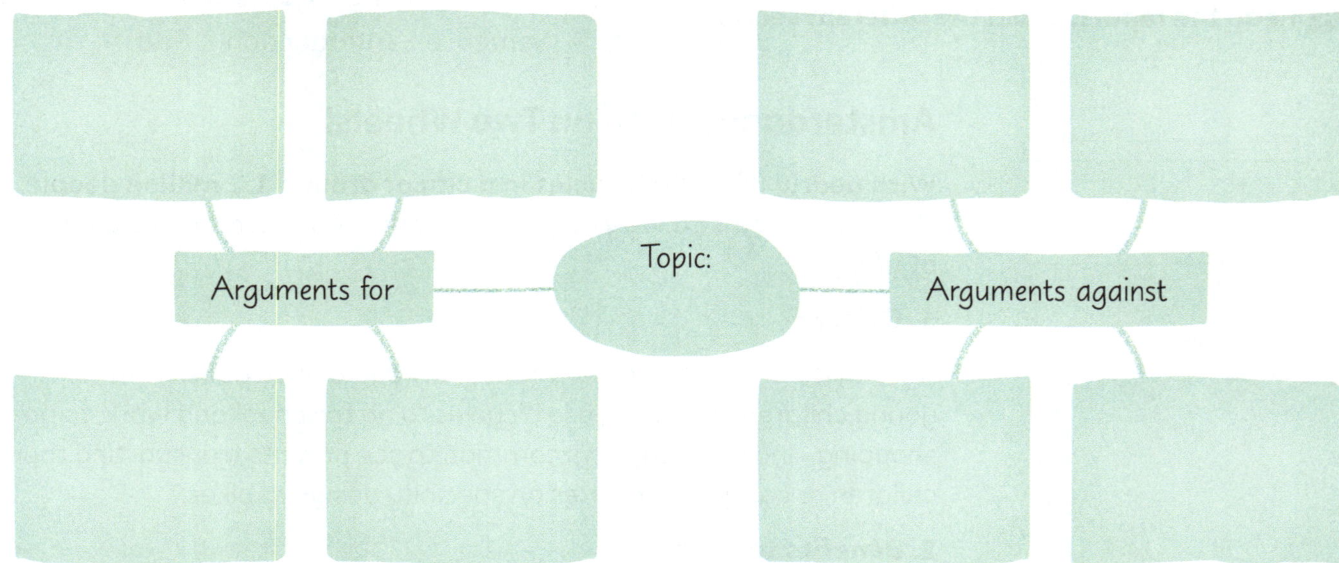

D Outline your ideas by completing the chart.

Topic:

Introduction:

Arguments for:	Arguments against:

Conclusion:

E Now write the first draft of your opinion essay in your notebook. 

- Write a short introduction to explain what the essay is about and give your personal opinion.
- Include arguments for and against, in separate paragraphs.
- Use topic sentences to start your for and against paragraphs.
- Use expressions such as *In my opinion*, *I think that*, or *I believe that*.
- In your conclusion, state your personal opinion about the topic.

F Check your work and make any necessary changes.

- Did you do everything in the list in **E**?
- Is your grammar, spelling, and punctuation correct?
- Is your writing clear and easy for other people to understand?

G Now write the final draft of your opinion essay in your notebook.

Report

A **Read the report. Label the different sections.**

Image   Heading   Caption   Topic
Sentence   Introduction   Title

____

____

____

____

____

Amsterdam: A City on Two Wheels!

With nearly 900,000 bicycles in a city of around 1.2 million people, cycling is not just a way of getting around Amsterdam; it's a way of life.

1. Culture

Cycling is part of Amsterdam's culture. People of all ages, from young children to seniors, use bicycles to go to school and work, to go shopping, and for leisure. It's common to see parents transporting their children or carrying groceries on specially designed bikes.

2. Benefits to people

The people of Amsterdam know that there are many benefits to cycling. Cycling is an excellent form of exercise that helps people's physical and mental well-being. Also, people can save money because they don't have to pay for gas, parking, or public transportation.

3. Benefits to the environment

Bicycles don't need gas, so cycling helps to reduce air pollution and fight climate change. Amsterdam experiences less traffic congestion than many other big cities thanks to bicycles. This also means that noise pollution is kept to a minimum and green spaces are protected.

4. Convenience

With its bike lanes, parking, and cycling tracks, Amsterdam has become a world leader in sustainable transportation. Bike lanes and cycle tracks help to keep people safe from cars and trucks. There are also a lot of special parking areas for the city's many bikes.

Bicycles parked in Amsterdam

Amsterdam is a model for cities around the world that want to encourage cycling as an efficient type of transportation that also provides health benefits for the people that live there.

B **Answer the questions.**

1   How does the writer start the report? ___________________________

2   How do the images help us to understand the report? ___________________________

3   How does the writer organize the information? ___________________________

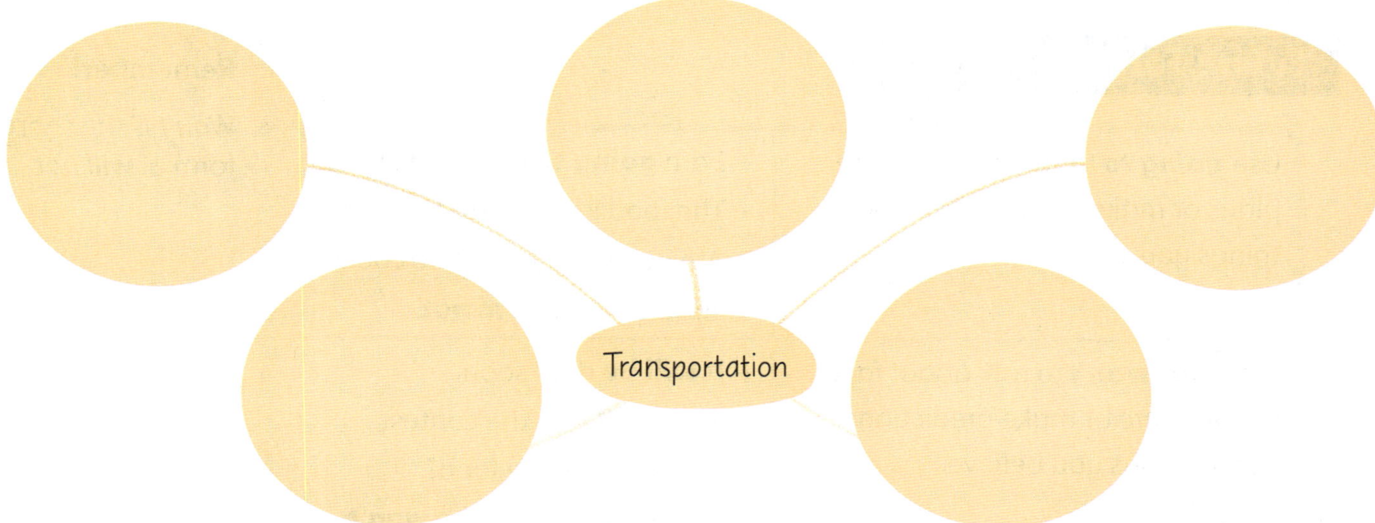

C You're going to write a report about transportation. Brainstorm. Write your ideas in the graphic organizer below.

D Outline your ideas by completing the chart.

Title:

Introduction:

Heading 1:	Heading 2:	Heading 3:
Information:	Information:	Information:

Visuals and captions:

E Now write the first draft of your report in your notebook. 

- Include a title that clearly states the topic and gets people interested.
- Start your report by giving some background information about the topic.
- Use images to help show the information in your report. Think about the captions that will explain what the visuals are.
- Organize your report into sections with headings so it's easier to understand.
- Include a topic sentence at the start of each main section.

F Check your work and make any necessary changes.

- Did you do everything in the list in **E**?
- Is your grammar, spelling, and punctuation correct?
- Is your writing clear and easy for other people to understand?

G Now write the final draft of your report in your notebook.

Grammar Reference

Unit 1

Future Forms (Review)

Use *going to* to talk about future plans or make predictions about things you see.	+ I am **going to buy** some herbs. - The food is**n't going to burn**. ? Are you **going to bake** cookies? Yes, I **am**. / No, I**'m not**.
Use *will* / *won't* to talk about facts in the future or make predictions about things you believe.	+ It **will be** dark soon. - We **won't win** the contest. ? **Will** she **like** the food? Yes, she **will**. / No, she **won't**.
Use the **present continuous** to talk about future arrangements, especially when you mention a specific time or place.	+ We **are meeting** at the park at 4:00 p.m. - He **isn't coming** to the meal tonight. ? **Am** I **playing** in the soccer game tomorrow? Yes, I **am**. / No, I**'m not**.

Unit 2

Continuous Tenses (Review)

Use the **present continuous** to say that something is in progress now.	+ A kingfisher **is flying** along the river. - I **am not preparing** for a race now. ? **Are** they **wearing** sharkskin swimsuits? Yes, they **are**. / No, they **aren't**.
Use the **past continuous** to say that something was in progress at a certain time in the past.	+ I **was waiting** for two hours. - You **weren't watching** the race. ? **Was** the cheetah **running** fast? Yes, it **was**. / No, it **wasn't**.
Use the **present perfect continuous** to say that someone started doing something in the past and they're still doing it.	+ They **have been studying** termites. - The cooling system **has not been working**. ? **Have** you **been improving** your design? Yes, I **have**. / No, I **haven't**.

Unit 3

Future Continuous

Use **future continuous** forms to talk about actions in progress at a future time.

will / won't + **be** + **-ing** form	**am / is / are** + **going to** + **be** + **-ing** form
+ We **will be cooking** when you arrive. - She **will not be celebrating** her birthday tomorrow. ? **Will** you **be sleeping** at 10:00 p.m.? Yes, I **will**. / No, I **won't**.	+ They **are going to be flying** to the U.S.A. at this time next week. - He **is not going to be reading** a book. ? **Are** you **going to be watching** a movie? Yes, I **am**. / No, I'**m not**.

Unit 4

Defining Relative Clauses for People and Objects

Relative clauses add extra information to a sentence. Defining relative clauses tell you important information about the noun.

They helped the girl who was carrying the box.

who was carrying the box is a defining relative clause. It tells you important information about the girl. Without it, you don't know which girl they helped.

We did an exercise which improves balance.

which improves balance is a defining relative clause. It tells you important information about the exercise. Without it, you don't know what kind of exercise we did.

Who, *that*, and *which* are relative pronouns.

To introduce **a relative clause about people**, you can use *who* or *that*.

Leo is the boy who / that can walk on his hands.

To introduce **a relative clause about living things**, use *that*.

Bonobos are monkeys that often walk on two legs.

To introduce **a relative clause about objects**, you can use *which* or *that*.

I don't want a lamp which / that falls over.

> **Remember!**
>
> Defining relative clauses are **not** separated by commas.

Unit 5

Defining Relative Clauses for Places and Possession

To introduce **a relative clause about a place**, you can use the relative pronoun **where**.

That's the beach where we found beautiful shells.

This is the place where we slept during the storm.

To introduce **a relative clause about possession**, you can use the relative pronoun **whose**.

Tiwa is the girl whose hut we liked.

Tiwa's mom is the person whose fishing skills helped us.

Usually, we use *my, your, his, her, its, our,* or *their* to show possession. These words tell you who something belongs to.

In a relative clause we use **whose** instead of *my, your, his, her, its, our,* or *their*.

I met a girl. *Her* family is from Chile. → **I met a girl whose** family is from Chile.

Compare **who** and **whose**.

I talked to a boy who lives in Toronto. (*He* lives in Toronto.)

I talked to a boy whose grandmother lives in Toronto. (*His* grandmother lives in Toronto.)

> **Remember!**
>
> Use defining relative clauses to give important information about a **noun** in a sentence.

Unit 6

Nondefining Relative Clauses

> **Tip**
>
> Nondefining relative clauses are more often used in writing than in speech.

Nondefining relative clauses give extra information about a noun in a sentence. Use commas to separate the nondefining relative clause from the rest of the sentence.

Katrina, who lives near a national park, did some research on the wolves in the park.

who lives near a national park is a **nondefining relative clause**. It tells you extra information about the person, object, or place identified in the sentence (in this example, the person, Katrina).

If you remove the nondefining relative clause, the sentence still makes sense.

Katrina did some research on the wolves in the park.

You can use **who**, **which**, and **where** in nondefining relative clauses, but not **that**.

Dr. Chan, who is an expert on orangutans, told us about the conservation plans.

The tiny leopard cub, which looked very young, was trying to climb a tree.

Bluestone Mountain, where I first saw the wolf, is a beatiful place.

Unit 7

Modals of Ability, Permission, and Request

Tip

These modal verbs have the same form after *I, you, he, she, it, we,* and *they.*

Ability

To talk about someone's skills and abilities (what they are and aren't able to do): in the **present**, use *can / can't*. in the **past**, use *could / couldn't* or *was / wasn't able to*. in the **future**, use *will / won't be able to*.	I **can't** ski. When I was seven, I **could** do handstands. I **wasn't able to** do somersaults. **Will** robots **be able to** explore the ocean floor?

Permission

To ask for permission (if you are allowed to do something), use *can, may,* or *could*.	**Can** I sit here? **May** I borrow your snorkel? **Could** we go inside the cave?

Requests

To make a request (ask someone to do something), use *can, could,* or *would*.	**Can** you hold my flashlight? **Could** you drive me to the beach? Please **would** you help me fix my surfboard?

Unit 8

Modals of Obligation, Possibility, and Deduction

Obligation

To talk about obligation (what's necessary): in the **present**, use *must, have to,* or *need to*. in the **past**, use *had to*. in the **future**, use *must* or *will have to*.	I **must** remember to wear suntan lotion. Last year, we **had to** organize a charity day at school. **Will** we **have to** give prizes?

Possibility

To talk about possiblity (what's possible), use *may, might,* or *could*.	It **may** rain later. / It **could** rain later. We **might** see a rainbow.

Deduction

To make a deduction (how sure we are about something), use *must* or *can't*.	You eat an apple every day. You **must** like apples. It's 1:00 p.m. It **can't** be dark yet.

Unit 9

Past Perfect

When you talk about something that happened in the past, you sometimes want to refer back to something that happened before that time. For this earlier action, you use the **past perfect**.

When we arrived, the parade had already started.

(First the parade started. Then we arrived.)

When we use the past perfect and the **simple past** together, we use the past perfect for the action that happened first and the simple past for the action that followed. The order of the actions in the sentence isn't important.

He had been ill during the night, so he stayed home in the morning.

He stayed home in the morning after he had been ill during the night.

(First he was ill. Then he stayed home.)

We make the past perfect with *had* + **past participle**.

+ She **had** already **gone** home by the time of the dragon dance.

- We were hungry because we **hadn't had** any lunch.

? **Had** you **known** about the festival before you came to Thailand? Yes, I **had**. / No, I **hadn't**.

Unit 10

Passive Statements (Present Perfect)

You can use the passive voice in the simple present and simple past. You can also use it in the present perfect to describe things that have happened up to now.

Active	Passive
have / has + past participle	*have / has* + *been* + past participle
+ Someone **has done** it.	+ It **has been done**.
- The soccer coach **hasn't chosen** them.	- They **haven't been chosen**.

You can often say the same thing using the active voice and the passive voice.

My teacher has started a photography club. (active)

A photography club has been started by my teacher. (passive)

In the active sentence, the focus is on the teacher. In the passive one, the focus is on the club.

Use the passive when it isn't important to say who does the action: **The evidence has been examined.**

To say who has done the action, use *by*: **The evidence has been examined by scientists.**

Unit 11

Passive Questions (Present Perfect)

You can ask **present perfect** questions in the active voice or the passive voice.

Active	Passive
have / has + subject + past participle	**have / has** + subject + **been** + past participle
? **Have** people **taken** photos of Saturn's rings? Yes, they **have**. / No, they **haven't**. ? **Has** the astronomer ever **seen** the comet? Yes, she **has**. / No, she **hasn't**.	? **Have** photos **been taken** of Saturn's rings? Yes, they **have**. / No, they **haven't**. ? **Has** the comet ever **been seen** by the astonomer? Yes, it **has**. / No, it **hasn't**.

Unit 12

Passive (Past Perfect)

You can use the **past perfect** tense in the active voice or the passive voice.

Active	Passive
had + past participle	**had** + **been** + past participle
+ Someone **had drawn** pictures. - The wind **hadn't blown** the pollen there. ? **Had** people **dropped** tools in the river? Yes, they **had**. / No, they **hadn't**.	+ Pictures **had been drawn**. - The pollen **hadn't been blown** there by the wind. ? **Had** tools **been dropped** in the river? Yes, they **had**. / No, they **hadn't**.

Unit 13

Passive (Future)

You can use **will** in the active voice or the passive voice to talk about the future.

Active	Passive
will + infinitive	**will** + **be** + past participle
+ They **will buy** a bassinet. - People **won't hear** the baby. ? **Will** Mom and Dad **cook** the dinner? Yes, they **will**. / No, they **won't**.	+ A bassinet **will be bought**. - The baby **won't be heard**. ? **Will** the dinner **be cooked**? Yes, it **will**. / No, it **won't**.

Unit 14

Passive (Review)

Simple Present Passive for things that are done in the present *am* / *is* / *are* + past participle	+ The cliff **is hit** by waves all day. - Boats **aren't damaged** by water. ? **Am** I **covered** in mud?
Simple Past Passive for things that were done in the past *was* / *were* + past participle	+ The village **was destroyed** in the storm. - The villagers **weren't hurt**. ? **Were** you **made** homeless?
Present Perfect Passive for things that have been done before the present *have* / *has* + *been* + past participle	+ New homes **have been built**. - The old village **hasn't been forgotten**. ? **Has** the wall **been weakened**?
Past Perfect Passive for things that had been done before some time in the past *had* + *been* + past participle	+ They **had been defeated**. - I **hadn't been told** about the storm. ? **Had** the work **been finished**?
Future Passive for things that will be done at or before some time in the future *will* + *be* + past participle	+ I **will be invited**. - Decisions **won't be made**. ? **Will** the work **be done**?

Unit 15

Zero, First, and Second Conditionals (Review)

We use the **zero conditional** to talk about situations.

If children go to school, they learn to read and write.

Situation: *if* / *when* + simple present

What happens: simple present

We use the **first conditional** to talk about things that are possible and likely in the future.

If we waste less food, we will help the planet.

Possible / Likely situation: *if* + simple present

Result: *will* + infinitive

We use the **second conditional** for things that are unreal now, or unlikely in the future.

If they became rich, they would buy a new house.

Unreal / Unlikely situation: *if* + simple past

Result: *would* + infinitive

Unit 16

Third Conditional

We use the **third conditional** to talk about past situations that didn't happen. You imagine that a situation happened in a different way.

If she had been there, she would have helped you.

There is an *if* clause and result clause: **if** + **past perfect** and **would have** + **past participle**

The order of the clauses doesn't matter. When the *if* clause is first, you need a comma after it. There is no comma when the result clause is first.

If we had run, we would have caught him.   **We would have caught him if we had run.**

Unit 17

If Only and I Wish

For how you would / wouldn't like things to be in the present, use: **if only** / **I wish** + simple past

If only my family liked the same food as me. (but sadly they don't like the same food)

I wish I didn't need to do the dishes! (but sadly I need to do the dishes)

To express a regret about the past, use: **if only** / **I wish** + past perfect

I wish we had remembered to buy some salmon. (but sadly we didn't remember)

If only he hadn't put nuts in the cookies! (but sadly he put nuts in the cookies)

Unit 18

Review of Present and Past Tenses

Use the …

simple present for routines, facts, habits, and schedules.	She **works** at the hospital.
present continuous for things in progress and future arrangements.	We **are raising** money for charity.
simple past for finished events in the past.	We **sold** toys at a bazaar.
past continuous for actions in progress in the past.	He **was waiting** for hours.
present perfect for things that have happened up to now.	They **have planted** six trees.
present perfect continuous for things that started in the past and continue up to now.	They **have been planting** trees all day.
past perfect for a past action that happened before another past action.	I **had finished** my homework before I started the game.

Irregular Verbs

Base Form	Simple Past	Past Participle
be	was / were	been
become	became	become
begin	began	begun
bend	bent	bent
bite	bit	bitten
break	broke	broken
breed	bred	bred
bring	brought	brought
build	built	built
buy	bought	bought
catch	caught	caught
choose	chose	chosen
come	came	come
cost	cost	cost
cut	cut	cut
deal	dealt	dealt
do	did	done
draw	drew	drawn
drink	drank	drunk
drive	drove	driven
eat	ate	eaten
fall	fell	fallen
feed	fed	fed
feel	felt	felt
find	found	found
fit	fit	fit
fly	flew	flown
get	got	gotten
give	gave	given
go	went	gone
grow	grew	grown
hang	hung	hung
have	had	had
hear	heard	heard
hide	hid	hidden
hit	hit	hit
hold	held	held
hurt	hurt	hurt
keep	kept	kept
know	knew	known
lead	led	led
leave	left	left
let	let	let
lie	lay	lain

Base Form	Simple Past	Past Participle
light	lit	lit
lose	lost	lost
make	made	made
meet	met	met
overcome	overcame	overcome
pay	paid	paid
put	put	put
quit	quit	quit
read	read	read
ride	rode	ridden
ring	rang	rung
rise	rose	risen
run	ran	run
say	said	said
see	saw	seen
sell	sold	sold
send	sent	sent
set	set	set
show	showed	shown
shut	shut	shut
sing	sang	sung
sink	sank	sunk
sit	sat	sat
sleep	slept	slept
speak	spoke	spoken
spend	spent	spent
stand	stood	stood
steal	stole	stolen
stick	stuck	stuck
stink	stank	stunk
sweep	swept	swept
swim	swam	swum
take	took	taken
teach	taught	taught
tear	tore	torn
tell	told	told
think	thought	thought
throw	threw	thrown
understand	understood	understood
wake up	woke up	woken up
wear	wore	worn
win	won	won
write	wrote	written